Opening Up
EPHESIANS

PETER JEFFERY

EVANGELICAL PRESS

Solid Ground Christian Books

Joint publication with

SOLID GROUND CHRISTIAN BOOKS
PO Box 660132, Vestavia Hills, AL 35266
205-443-0311 ~ http://www.solid-ground-books.com
e-mail: solid-ground-books@juno.com

and

EVANGELICAL PRESS
Faverdale North Industrial Estate
Darlington, DL3 0PH, ENGLAND
web: http://www.evangelicalpress.org
e-mail: sales@evangelicalpress.org

First published in May 2002

Opening Up Ephesians
Peter Jeffery

*Special thanks to Mr. Josh Priola for approaching the publisher
with the idea of a series of commentaries for young people. It is due
to his vision and passion for God's truth that this series has begun.*

ISBN: 0-9710169-7-6

Cover design: Peter Cooper

Manufactured in the United States of America

Contents

Author's Preface

I am very happy that you have picked up this book to take the first step in a journey through Paul's wonderful letter to the Ephesians. I am praying that God will use this book for whatever he has in store for your life.

This is not a commentary on Ephesians, but, as the title suggests, an attempt to *open up* the message of Ephesians for hungry hearts. I have sought to apply it especially to the spiritual needs of young people, but it is hoped it will benefit all ages. For over 25 years I have been writing books mainly for those beginning the Christian life, and I have tried always to be accurate, simple and brief. A pastor once said that too many Christian writers forget that they are supposed to be feeding sheep and not giraffes! My aim is to put the cookies where you can reach them. There are some glorious cookies in Ephesians and it would be a terrible shame if you were unable to benefit from them. Even so, there will be times along the way you will need to stand on your toes.

Ephesians will challenge you particularly on two fronts. First, do you know anything of the great salvation spoken of in chapter 2, and second, if so, are you taking seriously the call to radical commitment that Paul expresses so powerfully in chapters 4-6? Ephesians is not for the faint-hearted or those who only want Christianity as a hobby to pick up and put down at will.

Over the years I have found in pastoring young people that some make a profession of faith that does not last very long. Don't be one of those. Let chapter 2 sink into your heart and mind and do not go on to chapter 3 until you can say with confidence that you are God's workmanship.

Many young people are genuinely saved and go on well with the Lord for a few years, but then they seem to stagnate. They become like spiritual wheel barrows, no good unless they are pushed. If you take chapters 4-6 seriously this will not happen. The battle is not easy, but the victory is assured if you keep your eyes fixed upon Jesus, the Author and Finisher of your faith.

When my grandson Jonathan was four, like all three or four year olds, he loved to be told stories. He could sit and listen for hours to all the well-loved old fairy stories and the ones made up especially for him. But if he were to be asked which story he wanted read first, the answer would always be, 'Jack the Giant-Killer.' So when the school took all the four-year-olds to see the pantomime, 'Jack the Giant-Killer', he was very excited. He sat in the theater next to his mother enjoying the color and fun of the occasion. All was well until the giant appeared on stage; then he literally jumped from his seat onto his mother's lap in fear.

He could listen all day to the story of the giant. He knew the details by heart. But when confronted with the 'real thing', he was terrified. Isn't that like many Christians? We all have to face what seem to be giants in our life – problems, weaknesses and sins that appear too great for us to cope with. We can talk to our Christian friends about them and listen to sermons on how to deal with them, but when they actually confront us we are terrified and the 'giant' triumphs yet again in our lives.

How can we become spiritual giant-killers? Do you remember the story of David and Goliath in 1 Samuel 17? The giant was very confident in his defiance of God's people. 'This day I defy the ranks of Israel! Give me a man and let us fight each other,' he said (verse 10). No one would take up the challenge because they were all paralyzed with fear. The size of Goliath terrified them.

The giants of today still shout their challenges at God's people. We all know them and, sadly, we often feel totally inadequate and retreat in fear. What shall we do? Let us follow the example of David, who said, 'You come against me with sword and spear and javelin, but I come against you in the name of the Lord God Almighty, the God of the armies of Israel, whom you have defied ... All those gathered here will know that it is not by sword or spear that the Lord saves; for the battle is the Lord's'.

The armor of God is given to us for just such battles. Without it you will flounder, but clothed in God's invincible armor you will be assured of victory.

Peter Jeffery

Introduction to the 'Opening Up' Series

In Luke 24:13-49 one of the most striking and memorable events of our Lord's earthly ministry is recorded. Two dejected and confused disciples are making their way back home after the events of the Passover weekend that culminated in the execution of the Lord Jesus. In their own words you can hear and even feel their despair: 'We had hoped that he was the one who was going to redeem Israel' (verse 21). It appeared to them that their hope was all gone when suddenly the Resurrected Savior entered the scene and transformed their gloom into glory.

At the heart of this encounter the Lord rebukes the disciples (who are not aware of his identity), and then takes them on a never-to-be-forgotten journey through the Old Testament. We are told by Luke that 'Beginning with Moses and all the Prophets he explained to them what was said in all the Scriptures concerning himself' (verse 27). Some time later that evening after the Lord revealed who he was, and immediately disappeared, they said to each other, 'Were not our hearts burning within us while he talked with us on the road and opened the Scriptures to us?' (verse 32). They were never the same after that experience.

This new series of books on the New Testament derives its title from this Scripture. Our burden is to have the Word of God 'opened' for young people with the result that they will join the army of those with burning hearts. Each author is being selected for this series because he has been a proven instrument in the hand of Christ to open the Scriptures in a faithful and passionate way to lead people of all ages to love Jesus Christ.

This series is intended especially for young people, yet we hope it will reach a wider audience as well. It is hoped that it will prove useful for Sunday School and Bible Classes for older teenagers and adults, and for personal study as well. May the Lord bless the efforts being made to equip tomorrow's leaders in the home, church, school, workplace, armed forces and nation. To God alone be all the glory!

How to Get the Most out of this Book

You are invited to read this brief page before beginning your journey through Ephesians. Here are six simple suggestions that will help you to get the most out of your time spent:

1) Before reading the first chapter of this book be sure that you read the *entire* Epistle to the Ephesians. It is the inspired, inerrant word of God. It alone has the power to transform your life.

2) You may consider reading one chapter of Ephesians each day from Monday to Saturday, and the entire letter each Lord's Day. If you faithfully follow this plan you will find that this letter will become a bosom friend for life.

3) As you approach the chapter for the week be sure to have your Bible opened as you read the exposition. It will help you to follow along in the Bible as it is quoted.

4) At the end of each chapter you will find a section entitled: *Questions to Think about.* You are urged to take advantage of this material. Consider acquiring a notebook into which you can write the answers to the questions in this book. In addition to the questions following each chapter there is a section at the end of the book (pp. 85-99) called *Digging Deeper into Ephesians.* This material is intended for those who want to search the Bible for more information concerning the subjects covered in this book.

5) Be on guard against an *intellectual* approach to your study. While we must use our whole minds in our study of the word, we must remember that this is a *spiritual* exercise, and our profit will only be lasting if it is approached in a spiritual way.

6) Finally, seek to put into practice those things that the Lord opens up to you each time. We are told that Ezra, that great man of God, 'had devoted himself to the study and observance of the Law of the Lord, and to teaching its decrees and laws in Israel' (Ezra 7:10). Notice that he set his heart not only to 'study' but also to do the Law of the Lord. Only as we trust and obey will we grow in the Lord each day, and we were born to grow.

'*The Epistle to the Ephesians is the poem among the Epistles*'.
Benjamin B. Warfield

'*The Epistle to the Ephesians is a complete body of divinity,
treating of doctrinal, experimental, and practical godliness,
in a most full and instructive manner*'.
Charles H. Spurgeon

'*It is useless to try to attain the lofty ideal of conduct
in Ephesians 4 to 6, without attending to the heavenly vision
in Ephesians 1 to 3; just as on the other hand the vision itself grows
faint and disappears unless it is made effective
in holy living from day to day*'.
J. Gresham Machen

'*Some have observed that what the Apostle wrote
when he was a prisoner had the greatest relish and savor
in it of the things of God. When his tribulations did abound
his consolations and experiences did much more abound*'.
Matthew Henry

'*If Romans is the purest expression of the gospel,
Ephesians is the sublimest and the most majestic...
It emphasizes throughout the glory and greatness of God*'.
D. Martyn Lloyd-Jones

'*The letter to the Ephesians is a marvelously concise,
yet comprehensive, summary of the Christian good news.
Nobody can read it without being moved to wonder and worship,
and challenged to consistency of life. It was John Calvin's favorite*'.
John R.W. Stott

SUMMARY OF EPHESIANS

Paul spent three years at Ephesus (AD 54-57) and he obviously had a great love for this church which he had founded. It is not surprising, therefore, that during his imprisonment at Rome (AD 61-63), his thoughts turn to those saints and he writes to them this most beautiful letter.

The church at Ephesus was like any other church in that it had its problems, but at the time this epistle was written, there appeared to be no major difficulty and the letter is more general than, for instance, Galatians. Some think it was a circular letter sent to Ephesus and other churches in the area. As Ephesus was the capital of the Roman province of Asia, this is quite possible. The fact that it was not written to deal with any particular problem perhaps gives Ephesians a special value, as it presents to us basic Christianity.

The epistle to the Ephesians presents us with a worthy and exalted view of God. Paul starts by describing himself as being an apostle 'by the will of God'. But he does not stop there. If we are Christians, it is only because God chose us (1:4), predestined and adopted us (1:5). Our redemption is 'according to his good pleasure' (1:9). God works to a set purpose (1:9), to a plan which embraces everything (1:11), and our salvation is ultimately 'for the praise of his glory' (1:12).

Chapter 2 is one of the greatest statements of the gospel in the New Testament. The contrast between the first three verses and the last four is quite amazing. The opening verses describe what the Ephesians were before they became Christians. Deadness, hopelessness and helplessness are the condition of all in sin. How different are verses 19-22! 'You are no longer' like that, says Paul. The transformation is almost unbelievable. What has caused it? The bridge between these two extreme conditions is verses 4-18, the grace of God.

The Christian is God's workmanship (v. 10); faith is the result of God's mercy, grace and love working in our lives. There is no other possible explanation for the transformation that takes place at conversion. The gospel brings men into a state of peace with God and breaks down ancient barriers that separate man from man (vv. 14-18). Peace is established between those who were enemies because both have been reconciled to God by the blood of the Lord Jesus Christ.

The wonder of all this moves Paul in chapter 3 to pray for the Ephesians. Notice the phrase 'for this reason' in verses 1 and 14. He starts to say something in verse 1, then he stops and digresses for a while (vv. 2-13) before he comes back to his original thought in verse 14. This is not unusual in Paul's writings. He often goes off on a bypass before coming back to his main thought, but there is always a valid reason. The reason here is given in verse 13. Paul is writing this letter as a prisoner and he is concerned that the Ephesian Christians should not be discouraged by this. He encourages them by reminding them that though he is in a Roman prison, he is no prisoner of Rome but a prisoner of Jesus Christ (cf. 3:1; 4:1). In other words, God is still in control of the situation, despite the appearances. He uses the same sort of argument to the Philippians (1:12-18).

Summary of Ephesians

The prayer for the Ephesians (3:14-21) is prompted by the greatness of God's grace already shown to these Christians in the salvation already described. But no matter how much of the grace of God we have experienced, there is always more. The gospel does so many great things for us that Paul's application of it to the Christian is that we should live a life worthy of the grace of God. This he spells out in the remaining three chapters.

Notice the strength of the language in 4:17: 'So I tell you this and insist on it in the Lord, that you must no longer live as the Gentiles do.' He is insisting that the great transformation indicated in chapter 2 be evidenced by a change of attitude and behavior. The Christian is no longer in darkness; therefore he is to live as a child of the light (5:8). This means doing what pleases the Lord (5:10).

The Christian life is impossible without an experience of the great truths expounded in the first three chapters, but even then it is not easy and demands effort on our part. This effort is twofold. Firstly, it involves a putting off of the old self and its habits (4:22). We do this by rejecting the approaches of sin and by saying 'No!' to it (4:25-31). We are not to wait for something to happen to us; we are to 'get rid' of sin. There is not to 'be even a hint' of sin in our lives (5:3). Secondly, we are 'to put on the new self' (4:24). This we do by promoting the fruit of the light (5:9) in our lives. Paul works these things out in the specific relationships that most of us know: wives and husbands, children and parents, workers and employers. These are all to be affected by the filling of the Spirit (5:18).

The Christian life is not easy. In fact, it is a battle, and the great enemy, the devil, is ever vigorous in his opposition. So the Christian needs the armor of God (6:10-17). God supplies the armor, every piece, but we are responsible to put it on.

Paul's teaching on the armor of God does not finish with verse 17; he immediately goes on to show us how vital prayer is in the battle. Even though prayer is not a part of the armor, it is indispensable to the success of the armor.

Paul then concludes this powerful letter with some personal words of instruction and encouragement (6:21-24). As was his custom, he seeks for them all 'peace ...love with faith, from God the Father and the Lord Jesus Christ.' May these three be your portion as you begin to study this precious epistle.

1

A Fanfare of Truth

Ephesians 1:1-14

INTRODUCTION (1:1-2)

In verse 1 Paul commences the letter by stating his credentials for writing – 'by the will of God'. If this were not so we would be wasting our time reading Ephesians. We are living in a world where many voices are calling out for our attention, and this is particularly true of young people. Teenagers are seen as a market to exploit, but God sees them as young lives he wants to mold and direct. It is not exploitation but love and purpose that God wants to give you. Therefore to young people, especially young Christians, the supreme thing is to know God's will for your life. In Ephesians you will find principles of grace and living that will thrill you, satisfy you, challenge you and prove to be an infallible guide to discovering God's will for you.

Paul says four things about a Christian in verse 1:

- He is a saint
- He is faithful
- He is in Christ
- He is in Ephesus (or wherever you happen to live)

We have allowed the Roman Catholics to hijack the word 'saint' to mean a very special person who is recognized to be so much better than others. That is not how the New Testament uses the word. All Christians are saints – special to God and chosen by him alone. The word means to be set apart by God and for God, and the proof that this is true of any individual is that he or she is faithful to Christ. But it only can be true, as Dr. Lloyd-Jones says, because 'A Christian is one who believes certain specific truths; and the essence of his belief centers on the Person of our Lord Jesus Christ. The Christian, the saint, is "full of faith". But in whom, or what? Faith in the Lord Jesus Christ! He believes that Jesus of Nazareth was the only begotten Son of God. He is full of faith in the Incarnation, he believes that the Eternal "Word was made flesh and dwelt among us", that the Eternal Son came in human nature into this world; he believes in the Virgin Birth, and that Jesus manifested that he was the Son of God by his miracles'.

To be 'in Christ' means to be one with him, to love him and to trust him. It means to rely only upon him for salvation. It means that you are a part of him and he is a part of you. It speaks of an amazing and unique relationship Christ has with all his people forever. We will see more of this great truth in the verses to come.

Christians are not only 'in Christ', they are also, for the time being, in this world – 'in Ephesus'. And wherever we live in this world we are to live for Christ's glory and honor.

It is to such people that Paul writes this letter. To anyone else much of what he has to say will not make sense, but if you are a Christian the letter is full of glorious truths that will thrill your heart.

RICH IN CHRIST (1:3-14)

To be a Christian is the greatest privilege possible for anyone. Some people imagine that to be a Christian means being miserable and losing out on the joys of life, but they could not be more wrong. We have blessings in Christ that are beyond belief – 'who has blessed us in the heavenly realms with every spiritual blessing in Christ' (v. 3). These blessings are spiritual. In other parts of Scripture we are told of material blessings that come to us as a gift from God, but here Paul is concerned to show us our spiritual blessings. An unbeliever may benefit from the material blessings of God (Matt. 5:45), but these spiritual blessings are to be had only in Christ. If a person is not a Christian he cannot have them; indeed he would not even value them.

Before he mentions the blessings Paul urges us to join him in praise and worship of God for his unspeakable goodness to us. The more praise is on our lips, the more we will appreciate these spiritual blessings in our hearts. The closer we are to God (and praise is an indication of this), the more we will delight in all we have in Christ. When a Christian stops praising the Lord it is because he has come to undervalue what God has done for him in Christ. Learn early on in your Christian life just how rich you are because of your salvation. Praise is not something worked up or contrived but the inevitable overflow of a heart enjoying the blessings of God. And the blessings mentioned here are not dependent upon circumstances, therefore our praise should not be dependent upon circumstances either. Your eternal election, adoption, redemption and forgiveness depend upon the grace of God; therefore they never vary; they never change or diminish; there are no degrees to them. Because this is true our praise should never vary either. You are as fully redeemed and just as saved when circumstances in your life go all wrong, as when life is smooth. So praise is always appropriate. The more you dwell upon these eternal realities in Christ, the less you will be affected by disappointment, and the more you will find a new song in your mouth, even praise to your God.

The opening verses of Ephesians are a fanfare of doctrinal truths that ought to thrill the heart of any believer. It is these truths that are the foundation of all the blessings we have in Christ, and they are true of every believer everywhere.

The blessing of election. 'He chose us in him [Christ] before the creation of the world' (v. 4). This blessing of election and predestination is mentioned again in verses 5 and 11. Election simply means that God saves specific individuals by his own sovereign will. Some Christians find it difficult to believe this because they think it would remove human responsibility and it would be unfair. Both objections are wrong. In fact, election is one of the most thrilling and humbling truths in Scripture. This is the first blessing mentioned because it is the foundation and first cause of every other blessing. If God had not chosen us from before the creation of the world we could not be adopted or redeemed; we could not be 'in Christ'. It is significant to note that the apostle does not argue for this doctrine, but makes it a matter of praise. Thus it should be for every true child of God.

The blessing of adoption. Adoption is a term that Paul borrowed from the Roman legal system of his day. In this system of law the adopted person was given the right to the name and property of the one who adopted him. From a position of not belonging and having no rights, he became a son with a father. His relationship and standing was changed, and this change was brought about at the instigation of the adopting father. In gospel terms this means that all Christians have been adopted. From being a nobody in this world we became children of the

King of kings. And this was all due to the grace and mercy of God. What sin makes impossible for us, adoption by God makes very possible. Aliens become sons, strangers become children, and enemies inherit all the blessings of God. In other words, our relationship to God has totally changed and it is no small matter. Indeed, as one godly man said, it is the very apex of grace and privilege.

The blessing of redemption. The Bible says that man is dead in sin. Another way Scripture describes man's spiritual condition is that he is in bondage or slavery to sin (Rom. 6:20; 2 Pet. 2:19). Just as the man who is spiritually dead needs regenerating, so the same man who is a slave to sin needs redeeming. To redeem means to set free from slavery by the payment of a ransom price. Jesus has paid the ransom price on our behalf and he has done it once and for all. The price was far beyond anything we could afford. This is why Peter says that we are not redeemed with silver or gold but with the precious blood of the Lamb of God (1 Pet. 1:18-19). Only Jesus could pay that price. He alone is the Redeemer of God's elect.

The blessing of the forgiveness of sins. To be forgiven all our sin by God is a staggering thing. When Christ redeemed us he dealt with every sin we have committed, or will commit in the future. God's forgiveness is complete. There is no sin so small that it does not need forgiveness and no sin so large that it cannot be forgiven. When the Bible says that the blood of Jesus Christ cleanses us from *all sin* it means just that. There may be sins we have forgotten, but God knows every one and his forgiveness covers them all. What an incredible blessing!

The blessing of wisdom and understanding. You may not feel very wise but this blessing has nothing to do with our intellect. It has more to do with our faith. It is the God-given ability to understand and appreciate the things of God. John

MacArthur says, 'It is not surprising that those who do not even recognize that God exists, much less trust and serve him, do not have the least idea of what life, the universe, and eternity are all about.' When God takes away sin, he does not leave us in a spiritual, moral and mental vacuum where we must then work things out for ourselves. He lavishes wisdom and insight on us according to the riches of his grace, just as he lavishes forgiveness on us according to those riches. The man without Christ may be brilliant in the natural realm, but he will be ignorant in spiritual things. Spiritual wisdom is only for those who are filled with the Spirit and walk in the Spirit.

The blessing of the seal of the Holy Spirit. MacArthur says that 'The sealing of which Paul speaks here refers to an official mark of identification that was placed on a letter, contract, or other important document. The seal was usually made from hot wax, which was placed on the document and then impressed with a signet ring. The document was officially identified with and under the authority of the person to whom the signet belonged. That is the idea behind our being sealed in Christ with the Holy Spirit of promise. The seal of God's Spirit in the believer signifies four primary things: security, authenticity, ownership and authority.' When we are saved the Holy Spirit takes up residence in our lives, and his work and presence are the proof and guarantee that we really are believers. He guarantees our inheritance. The Christian is not someone who is naive or gullible; he has the most glorious assurance possible, for what he believes is true and his hope of heaven is guaranteed.

Such blessings never lose their freshness or significance. You can enjoy them as a young person and in your retirement years. In fact, the older you get, the more precious these truths will become to you.

QUESTIONS TO THINK ABOUT

1) Why does the book of Ephesians deserve our serious attention? List four benefits you hope to derive from this book.

2) Consider four things Paul says about a Christian in verse 1. See how many you can add to this list in verses 3-14.

3) Using the material you have found in these verses, how would you prove to someone that being a Christian does not mean being miserable?

4) Why is praise so important in a believer's life?

5) Consider the role of the Father, the Son and the Holy Spirit in the work of redemption as set forth in these verses. Use these truths as fuel to assist you in worship of the living God.

2

Prayer for Fellow Believers

Ephesians 1:15-23

Paul had a very high regard for the church at Ephesus. He had a remarkable ministry there (Acts 19), but that was sometime ago and he depended now upon news to keep him up to date with what was happening to these saints. What he heard encouraged him. They had a right relationship with God and each other (v. 15). They were not a perfect church (there is no such thing), and they had their problems. Later in the letter he instructs them on how to handle false doctrine (4:14), and in 4:31-32 he has to urge them to a deeper love for each other. But these things did not change the general picture of the Ephesians church. Paul was not wearing rose-tinted glasses when he looked at them and he was aware of their problems, but neither was he blind to the work of grace being done in them by the Lord of glory.

PAUL'S PRAYER (1:16-19)

Sometimes we hear of faults in Christians and churches and because of this we write them off. We dismiss them as no good as we generalize about particular incidents. When we do this we fail to see the good that God is doing and to thank him for it. Paul's response to what he heard in Ephesus was to pray for them (v. 16). Prayer is the pre-eminent activity of the Christian. Without it everything else will soon degenerate into lifeless formality. Prayer puts God at the center of our thinking and actions, and it strengthens both us and the folk we pray for. When we pray we need to be clear to whom we are praying. In verse 17 Paul addresses himself to 'the God of our Lord Jesus Christ, the glorious Father'. His concept of God flowed out of his experience of Christ. It is Christ alone who makes God the Father known to us and such a view of God will encourage prayer because it gives a hope of the prayer being answered. What use are prayers which are merely the mouthing of words with our eyes closed? The power of prayer lies in the one to whom we pray.

Paul prays that the Ephesians may know God better. Now they already had a saving knowledge of God, but that was only the beginning. The prayer starts in verse 18. There is no knowledge of God without spiritual vision. In salvation our hearts are opened by God so that we may receive this, but now Paul is concerned that these Christians may have their hearts enlightened to receive more and more of Christ. They need to know 'the hope to which he has called you.' Dr. Lloyd-Jones says, 'He means our realisation that we have been called to these things and for these things. In other words it refers once more to assurance of salvation.'

Our salvation is not the result of someone's persuading us to become a Christian and of our making a wise decision to come to Christ. If that is all it is, others could dissuade us and we could decide to forget all about it. Salvation involves God calling us to himself. He does it. The hope or ground or basis of assurance is that God himself has called me personally. Salvation is God's work in our hearts, and what he has done no one can undo. We may not realize this fully at the time of our salvation, but we need to appreciate it soon afterwards because it opens to us 'the riches of his glorious inheritance in the saints'. To quote Lloyd-Jones again, 'It is a prayer that we may come to know something of that glorious state to which we are going, and for which God is preparing us, when with all the redeemed we shall be safely gathered in and shall enjoy for all eternity the benefits of this great salvation'.

To know this here and now will determine the sort of Christian life we will live. We can either be earthbound, seeing everything in relationship to the present, or we can live with one eye on eternity. We are sometimes warned not to be so heavenly-minded that we become no earthly good. But the greater danger for the believer is to be so earthly-minded that we are no good to God in fulfilling his work in this world here and now. It is those Christians who continually have an eternal perspective that are the greatest use in the church. An awareness of heaven is not only good for someone about to die, but also for a young person facing the temptations of everyday life. It can utterly transform your attitude to sin. For instance, would you be so keen to go clubbing or drinking if you thought of all that you have in Christ here and now, and what is waiting for you in heaven?

Paul is also concerned that we appreciate the enormity of the power that was needed to save us and keep us secure (v. 19). Love and grace save us, but supernatural power also has to intervene if the sinner is to be saved. Only the mighty hand of God can break the chains that bind us and bring us out of the prison of sin. This prayer is continually reminding us that it is God who saves, and it reinforces words like 'chosen' and 'predestined', which Paul has already used. If the power that saved us is likened to the power that raised Christ from the dead, then that puts our salvation firmly in the hands of God.

CHRIST EXALTED (1:20-23)

Paul had a great love for his Savior and often when writing about him he gets carried away in praise and adoration. He just delights in exalting Christ and he does so here in verses 20-23. Is your love for Christ like this? Does the gospel excite you? As a young believer are you thrilled about your relationship with Christ? When we are first converted the wonder of it thrills our souls (at least it ought to), but sadly this seems to wear off with many Christians. It did not with Paul. He was writing to the Ephesians many years after his conversion but still his heart delighted to exalt his Savior. Enthusiasm for Christ has nothing to do with age. You need to have your initial joy and thrill of salvation just as much, if not more, thirty years later as in the early days.

Salvation is not only a matter of grace and love but it also needs divine power. This is because of the reality of the control sin has over us, as Paul will describe in the opening verses of chapter 2. So complete is Satan's dominion over unsaved people that it will take immense power to break his hold. Such a power works for us. Paul describes it as an 'incomparably great power', and then goes to compare it with the power God exerted to raise Christ from the dead. Your salvation needed such power; so clearly then, salvation had to be all of God, because you had no power like this. It is as we realize this that we appreciate more and more the greatness of what God has done for us. Salvation is no small thing, easily accomplished with a little effort on our part. It is impossible without the infinite power of God, and Paul prays that we might be aware of this. In the New Testament a yardstick by which power is measured is always Christ's resurrection. There is nothing greater! Doesn't it thrill your heart to realize that God exerted such power just for your salvation?

This power exalted Christ from the weakness of his humiliation on the cross to the glory of the right hand of God. The phrase 'the right hand of God' speaks of power and authority, but it also speaks of love. When God set Christ down on his own right hand it indicated the great love he had for his Son. The extent of Christ's power and the wonder of his exaltation are brought out clearly in verses 21-23. If you think of any power in the universe – angelic or demonic – Christ's power is not only above these, but *far* above, indeed, infinitely above.

Paul prays that we know this because often we get dejected and perhaps doubt the ability of Jesus to meet our needs. We cower before the power of evil as it comes to tempt us. We see the power of sin obviously dominant in the world and we despair of good ever triumphing. We stand in awe at the power of the world compared to the weakness of the church. Then our heads fall and our knees buckle as we well-nigh accept defeat as inevitable. Christian teens find it difficult to cope with the pressures from their unbelieving friends and find it so easy to go with the crowd. Peer pressure can be overwhelming, and it does not stop when you leave your teens behind. So how are we to deal with these things? We are to remember the all-pervading power of Christ that is working for us. We are weak but our Savior is strong.

Do we believe that God is Almighty? We need to. It is no accident that the Old Testament verse quoted more often in the New Testament than any other is a verse which stresses this power of God. It is Psalm 110:1: 'The Lord says to my Lord: "Sit at my right hand until I make your enemies a footstool for your feet"'. It is only a great Savior who could provide a great salvation and there is none greater than Jesus!

What Paul has said so far about the exalted Christ is a great encouragement for us, but he does not stop there. Everything that Christ is, he is 'for the church' (v. 22). The church, you see, is no man-made institution that we can ignore if we want to. The church is God's idea. He brought it into being and ordained what it needs to be in this world. The church 'is his body' (v. 23). More than that it is described as 'the fullness' of Christ. There are various interpretations of what exactly this means and you can read these for yourself in the commentaries, but for a young person it will be enough at this point to grasp the importance of the church. Christ and the church, in the will and purpose of God, cannot be separated. So don't fall for the teaching that the church is of no consequence and each Christian can do his own thing irrespective of other believers. Each Christian needs the church and the church needs each Christian because this is the way God ordained it to be. John MacArthur says, 'As a head must have a body to manifest the glory of that head, so the Lord must have the church to manifest his glory (Eph. 3:10).'

QUESTIONS TO THINK ABOUT

1) Why is prayer so important for the Christian?

2) What is your reaction to the criticism that a Christian can be so heavenly-minded that he is no earthly good?

3) Why is it impossible to be saved without divine power?

4) Why do you think that Psalm 110:1 is quoted in the New Testament more than any other Old Testament verse?

5) How important should the church be to the Christian? Why do so many think they can follow Christ but neglect the church?

3

By Grace Through Faith

Ephesians 2:1-10

The Bible is a wonderful book. It is a reservoir full of glorious truths, but even in such a remarkable book there are certain passages which stand out. Chapter 2 of Ephesians is such a passage. The gospel is set before us as clearly here as anywhere else in the Bible and divine grace, love and mercy are shown to be the sinner's only hope.

CHRISTIANS BEFORE THEY ARE SAVED (2:1-3)

The people Paul are writing to are saints who lived in Ephesus. They were believers in the Lord Jesus Christ, but they were not always like that. When Paul first visited Ephesus in Acts 19 these people were very religious but far from being Christian. Ephesus was a famous religious center for the worship of Artemis (Acts 19:27,34). Religious or not, the Ephesians were, in God's sight, dead in sin.

The first three verses of chapter 2 are not a description a man would willingly give of himself. Indeed, if he is religious he will deeply resent these words, but this is how God regards all men and women outside of Jesus Christ. Human beings are:

- Dead in sin
- Enslaved by the devil
- Disobedient to God
- Sinful in his very nature
- Under the wrath of God

Here are five devastating facts about us all. No human being is outside the breadth of this description. Some are more aggressive in their sin than others, but all are sinners.

'*Dead in sin*' means simply what it says – dead. Paul is speaking of our spiritual condition, and spiritually we are either dead or alive. We cannot be half-dead. There are no degrees to this, and the fact that we are dead means that we cannot make any spiritual response to God. Man is utterly and completely helpless in the grip of sin and unable to do anything about it. 'Dead' must be one of the most absolute words in the English language (or any language for that matter). It allows for no variation and no improvement. You would not expect a man who is physically dead to enjoy a good meal or appreciate the beauty of the sunset. In the same way, a man who is spiritually dead can appreciate nothing of the truth of God. Until we see this we will never understand just how amazing the gospel really is.

Being spiritually dead is bad enough, but Paul doesn't stop there. He draws out what this means by asserting that we are *enslaved by the devil*. In other words, this spiritual condition of deadness is seen in how men and women live their lives. Verse 2 tells us that instead of being servants of God, we were slaves of the devil. This enslavement was not against our wills but with full cooperation of that will. We enjoyed sin – we gratified the cravings of our sinful heart. What Jesus told the unbelieving Jews of his day was true of us: 'You are of your father the devil' (John 8:44). What was true of us as Christians is now true of all who do not love and serve the Lord Jesus.

If a person is enslaved by the devil he will inevitably live a life that is in rebellion to God. *Disobedience to God* is the product of not loving God, even as love for God is shown by obeying him (John 14:15; 15:10,14). For the believer obedience is not simply a matter of following a set of rules. It is the loving response of the redeemed soul to his heavenly Father. An unbeliever can know nothing of this.

The problem all stems from *our sinful nature.* Man is born with a sinful, rebellious and disobedient nature. We are born rebels against God. Some object to this and point to a little baby, so innocent and beautiful. They say that sin is not in the child but in the world and it is the environment that the child grows up in which will lead him to sin, not his nature. But the Bible most emphatically contradicts this. Read what Jesus said in Matthew 15:11-20 and see his assessment of the human heart. Read again Romans 3:10-18 for the apostle's opinion, which is entirely based upon the Old Testament Scripture. Let us never forget that man first sinned in a perfect, sin-free environment (Gen. 3:1-8).

This nature of sin puts us all *under the wrath of God.* In other words, sins has its consequences. Judgement and eternal death are what the sinner deserves and what he will surely receive unless his sin is dealt with. We must never forget that while the Bible speaks to us about the love of God it also speaks about the holiness of God, and hence his righteous indignation against all sin. We are told that Jesus spoke more about hell than heaven while he was upon this earth. Has that fact sunk in?

SAVED BY GRACE (2:4-9)

It is a frightening picture that is presented to us in these first three verses. If all this is true, and it is, can there be any hope for us? How can anyone in such a terrible spiritual condition possibly be saved? It all seems so hopeless, and it is if salvation depended on our efforts.

The little word 'but' in verse 4 begins to give us hope. It suggests an answer to an unanswerable problem. The answer, put very simply, is that *salvation is God's work, not ours*: 'It is by grace you have been saved.' Saved is a great biblical word and means that the sinner can be delivered from the consequences of the condition described in verses 1-3. So then, how can a guilty sinner be saved?

In verses 4-9 Paul tells us very clearly and simply two things. First of all, there is the very positive statement that we are saved by grace. Then, so that this is clearly understood and to remove any possible misunderstanding, Paul adds an equally strong negative statement: 'not by works'; not of yourselves.

We are not saved from the guilt, power and consequence of sin by our own efforts. We cannot deal with our own sin. The opening three verses have made it very clear why this is so. Salvation by works totally fails to take into account the reality of these verses and also the reality of the holiness of God. It sees sin only as a moral or social blemish and not as an insult to the word, law and character of God. Because of this it always fails and therefore salvation must be by grace alone.

Grace is the undeserved favor of God. It is God doing for us what we do not deserve – he saves us. Grace is God working. It is God loving the ungodly, pardoning the guilty and saving the lost. Grace is the unique work of God.

Paul introduces us in verses 4-5 to three great words that all describe an activity of God – 'love', 'mercy' and 'grace'. Grace flows out of the love of God and fully satisfies his holiness. It does this because it supplies a complete answer to human sin. When grace begins to work it never forgets the absolute holiness of God; therefore it has to provide for the guilty sinner a salvation that does not gloss over sin or minimize its

effects. There must be no short cut to salvation and no mere
theoretical dealing with sin. God's holiness cannot be deceived
or satisfied with such things. The objective of grace is not
merely to make the sinner accept God, but to make it possible
for a holy God to have mercy on the sinner and accept him.

God does all this for us in and through his Son, the Lord Jesus
Christ. Firstly he makes us 'alive with Christ'. Spiritual life
has to be the remedy to the spiritual death that all men and
women are in because of their sinful nature. Dr. Lloyd-Jones
says, 'The Christian is not a man who is hoping to be
forgiven; the Christian is not a man who hopes that ultimately
he will be able to satisfy the demands of the law and to stand
before God. If he is a Christian who understands Christianity
he says, I am already there, I have ceased to be dead, I am
alive, I have been quickened, I have been made alive. The
Scriptures make this definite assertion; I am not a Christian,
I cannot be a Christian at all, without being in Christ. It
follows that if I am in Christ, what is true of him is also true
of me. He has died unto sin once, and I have died unto sin
once, in him'.

The purpose of salvation is not only that we should be
delivered from the consequences of our sin, but also that we
might begin here and now to enjoy the new life we have in
Christ. Paul deals with this in verses 6-7. John MacArthur tells
us, 'When Jesus raised Lazarus from the dead his first
instruction was "Unbind him, and let him go" (John 11:44). A
living person cannot function while wrapped in the trappings
of death. Because our new citizenship through Christ is in
heaven (Phil. 3:20), God seats us with him in the heavenly
places, in Christ Jesus... To be in the heavenly places is to be
in God's domain instead of Satan's, to be in the sphere of
spiritual life instead of the sphere of spiritual death'.

Are you beginning to appreciate that becoming a Christian is impossible without the grace of God? And can you see that it is far more than merely becoming religious? An explosion of grace takes place in the sinner's heart and mind that changes everything about his relationship with God.

So how do we benefit from grace? Verse 8 tells us that it is through faith, and even this faith is the gift of God. We are not saved *by* faith but *through* faith. Faith is the channel by which saving grace comes to us. Faith trusts in what God has done. It looks at the cross in wonder and amazement. It throws itself on the love and mercy of God, and comes to see that the only reason for the existence of faith is the grace of God. If there were no grace, faith would be useless. It is grace, not faith, that saves. As Jonah learned in the heart of the sea and the belly of the fish, 'Salvation is of the Lord' (Jonah 2:9).

GOD'S WORKMANSHIP (2:10)

Out of God's love comes mercy and grace. Mercy is God not giving us what we deserve. Grace is God giving us what we do not deserve. A Christian is God's workmanship. He is the result of the work and activity of God. Paul uses the word 'created' to show that when God was dealing with the problem of human sin he did not do a repair job. He made or created something new. A Christian is not a repaired sinner; he is a new creation in Christ. This is only possible if God creates Christians.

God takes the raw material of human nature, as described in verses 1-3, and does something staggering with it. Human nature is so twisted and warped, so full of flaws and knots, that it would take a workman of infinite skill to do anything with it. God is such a workman. There is no raw material that God cannot work with. This is our only hope, but it does mean that there is no one so deep in sin that they are beyond the reach of divine grace. No matter what the sin, God has the power and grace to deal with it.

Our own good works do not save us, but we are saved 'to do good works'. The evidence that a sinner is saved is that he now leads a new life to the glory of God. Paul is going to deal with this in depth in chapters 4-6, but let me illustrate what he is talking about.

When I was a student in college I spent two summers working for a local council, cutting grass in a cemetery. The man in charge of the cemetery had a strange dislike to anything Christian and lost no opportunity to attack my Christian faith. One day as we were working together, he pointed to a man walking through the cemetery and said, 'There's a man who was ruined by Christianity.' He went on to explain that during the Second World War that man was deeply involved in the local 'black market'. In the war years everyone had ration books; everything was in short supply and certain goods were virtually impossible to obtain. But the 'black market' men could get you anything – at a highly inflated price. I was told that this man was making a fortune selling goods on the 'black market'. 'He was raking it in,' said my foreman, 'but then he got converted and gave it all up. Christianity ruined him.'

What a marvelous, though unintentional, testimony to the power of the gospel! Paul says that when we become Christians, we become new creatures; old things pass away, all things become new. Christianity ruins us for dishonesty and greed. It breaks the power of sin. Christ gives us a new life with new ambitions, new desires and new standards. It ruins us for sin!

QUESTIONS TO THINK ABOUT

1) What does the phrase 'dead in sin' mean? How does Paul describe the condition of the person who is not a Christian?

2) Why do we enjoy sin so much?

3) Why is salvation by our own works so popular with many who call themselves Christians?

4) Define the word 'grace' in your own words. How does grace relate to the other two words used here: 'love' and 'mercy'?

5) Why would faith be useless without God's grace?

6) What is the proper place of good works for the Christian life? How does 2:10 help you answer this question?

4

One in Christ

Ephesians 2:11-22

It seemed that everything in the Ephesians' lives worked against their becoming Christians. The greatest barrier was their sinful condition. This condition is true of all people, but in their case there was another barrier – they were Gentiles (vv. 11-12). A Gentile is anyone who is not a Jew and this meant that they had none of the privileges a Jew had at that time. They had no Scriptures, no history of God dealing with them and no covenant promises. They were in this world 'without hope and without God'.

There are many things in our background that seem to work against our ever becoming Christians. Most young people in Britain today have never been inside a church and have no idea what the gospel is. While in America there are many more who have attended church, there are sadly few who have been confronted with an accurate presentation of the gospel and its demands. Too often young people are entertained in church and not challenged to radical discipleship. God and Jesus are remote concepts to young people today that seem totally irrelevant to modern life. How can such young people ever be saved?

THE BLOOD BRINGS PEACE (2:13-18)

In verse 13 we have another one of those great 'buts'. The Ephesians were so far removed from God in every conceivable way, that if salvation was not of grace, it would have been impossible. It is Jesus Christ who changes everything. His death on the cross brings sinners near to God in salvation. Notice that in verse 13 Paul does not mention directly the death of Jesus; rather he refers to the 'blood of Christ'. The word 'blood' is vital to a true understanding of salvation. The New Testament writers keep telling us that we are saved by the blood of Jesus (Acts 20:28; Rom. 3:25; 1 Pet. 1:19; 1 John 1:7). They are describing the death of Jesus in the language of the Old Testament sacrifices, and the point they are making is that it is not merely the death of Jesus that atones for sin, but his sacrificial death. He did not die of natural causes or of an accident, it was planned by God (Acts 2:22-24; 4:27,28). Jesus died as a sacrifice for our sins.

Tragically there are teachers in the church today who despise what they call 'bloody religion'. They desire to have the moral teaching of Christ without dealing with a bloody cross. This is a tragedy because 'without the shedding of blood there is no remission' of sin (Heb. 9:22, [NKJV]).

There are barriers which separate us from God and there are also barriers which separate us from each other. Jew and Gentile was, and still is, one of the most sensitive flashpoints in human relationships. But in Christ all that should disappear. John MacArthur says, 'The only solution for divisions among men is the removal of sin, which Jesus Christ accomplished by the shedding of his own blood... Because in Christ the great foundational barrier of sin has been removed, every other barrier has been removed as well. Those who are in Christ are one in each other – whether they realize it or act like it or not (1 Cor. 6:17). The purpose of the Lord's Table is to remind us of the sacrifice our Lord made not only to bring us to himself but also to each other. By removing our sin, Christ gives us peace with each other and access to God.'

In verses 14-17 Paul works out our oneness in Christ in terms of the peace that the Lord has brought us. If we have peace with God we should also have peace with all who belong to God. Jesus did not die so that there would be Jewish Christians and Gentile Christians, but that they should simply be Christians. The national tag is now totally irrelevant. In the same way whether we are young Christians or old Christians is also irrelevant. The age barrier disappears in Christ as does the national one. If a man is a Christian he is my brother, and not just in theory but in reality.

The hallmark of a Christian church should be peace, because Christ is our peace. And peace is not just the absence of war and hostility but the presence of love. If Christ is my peace and also the peace of others in the church, then he should be *our* peace. We have no right to be in conflict with one whom Christ loves and with whom he is at peace.

CONSEQUENTLY (2:19-22)

The difference between the opening three verses of this chapter and the closing four verses is amazing. It does not seem possible that these two sections are describing the same people. But they are, and the bridge between the two so different stages is the grace of God (vv. 4-18). Christ makes all the difference. The Ephesians are no longer what they were because now they are in Christ. What was true of them is true of every believer. We all have a before and after in our lives. When Christ became our Savior everything changed, and this change can clearly be seen by comparing verses 1-3 with verses

19-22. No change could be more dramatic and only God could cause it. Notice again the breakdown of the chapter.

- *Verse 1.* As for you...
- *Verse 4.* But... God...
- *Verse 19.* Consequently...

The opening verses describe the world; and the closing ones the church, and the difference between the world and the church is the grace of God. When the Ephesians were converted to Christianity in Acts 19 the immediate change in their lives was obvious (read Acts 19:18-20). They knew nothing of the current evangelical nonsense of receiving Jesus as Savior but not as Lord. They were new creatures in Christ. They were converted, changed, and the difference was clear.

As a young Christian get this sorted out in your mind. To have one foot in the world and one foot in the church is disastrous. It may be that older Christians have not set you too good an example in this, but your standard must be what the Bible says, not current whims and fancies. Today it is difficult at times to distinguish the church from the world. This happens when the church fails to appreciate what man is (2:1-3) and stops preaching what God has done to rectify this (2:4-18). When that happens the church ceases to have a gospel message, which is the thing above all others that distinguishes it from the world. At that point it has ceased to be what the New Testament means by a church.

If you have been saved the difference is there but you must let it shine out. Live out the difference so that everyone can see that you belong to Christ. Paul is going to spend the second half of Ephesians telling us this: 'I urge you to live a life worthy of the calling you have received' (4:1). There he will spell out in detail what this means, but now at the end of chapter two he is content to describe the difference in general but thrilling terms.

QUESTIONS TO THINK ABOUT

1) Why do the New Testament writers use the word 'blood' when referring to the death of Christ?

2) What is the relationship between being one in Christ and being at peace with each other?

3) Do you have a before and after in your life? List specific ways that God has changed your attitudes and lifestyle.

4) Some people teach today that it is possible to have Jesus as Savior and yet reject him as Lord. How can you show from Ephesians that this is not true?

5) Why is it disastrous to have one foot in the church and one foot in the world?

5

The Mystery Revealed

Ephesians 3:1-13

The glory and majesty of what Paul has been saying in the first two chapters is overwhelming. These are not theories but realities upon which to build your life. Paul certainly built his life upon the truth of the gospel so he was able to say, 'For this reason', or, in the light of all he has been saying, 'I, Paul, the prisoner of Christ Jesus' write to you.

He was writing from a prison in Rome where he was a prisoner of Caesar awaiting a possible death sentence. But he called himself a prisoner of Christ because he firmly believed that everything was under the control of the Lord Jesus Christ. What a blessed state of mind this man had and this was all because he actually believed all he had written and thus he based his life upon it. The gospel was not something that happened to him only on the road to Damascus (Acts 9); it was happening every day of his life. So everything that happened to him, even imprisonment, he saw as a means to further the gospel.

This should be true of all believers, but is it? Christian young people may groan and wish that they had better academic qualifications. If this was so they could get to go to a better college or have a better job. So for a while their whole life becomes unsettled and dissatisfied. Qualifications have taken the place of Christ as the center of their lives. Or perhaps it is a broken relationship, or failure on the athletic field, or poor health. These things are important but if they alone determine our state of mind then we have forgotten the glories of Christ. Paul never forgot what really matters, so even in a prison cell he sees opportunities to serve his Savior.

A BLESSED DIGRESSION (3:1)

You will notice that at the end of verse 1 Paul suddenly seems to stop. Dr. Lloyd-Jones says, 'He was obviously going to say something further, but he pauses, he hesitates, and he does not say it until he gets to verse 14, where we find exactly the same formula again – 'For this cause I' ['For this reason' NIV] – and then goes on to tell them that he is praying for them, and what he is praying for them. In other words, from verse 2 to the end of verse 13 we have a long digression... In this digression [or aside] the Apostle gives the Ephesians an account of his own ministry – his calling, his office – and its great object and purpose. Then, having done so, he comes back again to this theme and says what he was setting out to say in the first verse.'

THE MYSTERY REVEALED (3:2-13)

In verses 2-13 Paul deals with what he calls 'the mystery'. By definition a mystery is something hidden. Throughout the centuries there have been many mysteries which have been cleared up by man's ingenuity. For instance, medical problems which baffled doctors a hundred years ago are now common knowledge to medical people. But man can never know the mystery that Paul is speaking about unless it is revealed to him by God (vv. 5 and 10). This mystery is the gospel and in particular the great truth that it is for all men and women, Jews and Gentiles alike (v. 6).

In the Old Testament there are many hints as to the nature of the gospel and we can understand them now in the light of the full gospel revelation in the New Testament. But even such glorious passages as Isaiah 53 would have remained a mystery until Christ came and died on the cross. The Old Testament would still be a confusing book to us without the light we have in the New Testament. So the true nature of the gospel was a mystery and so too was its breadth. Even the first Christians in Acts 10 had difficulty in believing that the gospel was not only for Jews but also for Gentiles. James M. Boice says, 'It is true, of course, that God announced his intention of saving Gentiles as well as Jews from the beginning. But before the coming of Christ it was understood that this was to happen only as Gentiles became Jews through proselytizing. A Gentile could approach the God of Israel, but only as an Israelite. He had to become a member of the covenant people through the rite of circumcision. The new thing revealed to Paul is that this approach is no longer necessary. Christ has broken down that wall, making one new people out of two previously divided people. So now both Jew and Gentile approach God equally on that new basis'.

In verse 6, to stress the reality of this, Paul uses the word 'together' three times – 'heirs together... members together... sharers together'. Every redeemed sinner in Christ shares the same gospel privileges. In Christ the Jew is no more favored than the Gentile is. To us today this may be obvious, but to the Jewish Christians in the early church it was a completely new concept. It went against all the traditional Jewish teaching of the inferiority of the Gentiles. In Acts 10 and 11 it is very clear to see how hard this was for the Jews to accept. In the light of this, it was crucial that the church realized that the oneness of Jew and Gentile in Christ was no man-made doctrine but a revelation from God (vv. 2,3 and 5). This was part of God's 'eternal purpose' (v. 11). Paul became a servant of the gospel to preach to men and women 'the unsearchable riches of Christ' (v. 8). Paul had no high opinion of himself, in fact he saw himself as 'less than the least of all God's people' (v. 8). This was not false humility but, in the light of his actions before his conversion, his honest assessment of his worth. It was nothing but divine grace that made him anything of value to the church.

The unsearchable riches of Christ include the truths about Jesus from his incarnation to his Second Coming, and all the blessings these make available to Christ's redeemed people. Such things are only known by revelation from God. This final revelation of truth came first to Paul and the other apostles (v. 5) and is given to us through the Scriptures. If anyone wants to know the gospel he must go to the Bible. In the words of Dr. Lloyd-Jones, 'So we are entirely confined to the Scriptures, and we can add nothing to them. Neither must we take anything from them. We are in no position to pick and choose from them. We cannot say, "I believe this and I reject that. I rather like the teaching of Jesus, but do not believe in miracles; I admire the way in which he died, but I do not believe that he was born of a virgin or that he rose in the body from the grave". The moment you begin to do that you are denying revelation. You are saying that your unaided intellect is capable of judging revelation, and sifting it and finding what is true and what is false. That is to deny the whole principle of revelation, of the apostolate, and of this unique work of the Holy Spirit'. It is often a tendency for young people to be independent thinkers, but it is a foolish and tragic thing for you to think you know better than God. Take him at his word. It is your only safe guide for all time.

QUESTIONS TO THINK ABOUT

1) Paul considered himself a prisoner for Christ. How was he able to do this? Why does he speak this way for the sake of the Ephesian Christians? How does this apply to us today?

2) Why does Paul refer to the gospel as a 'mystery'? How does his use of this word differ from the common conception of the word 'mystery' in movies and novels in our day?

3) If you knew nothing of the New Testament how might you understand Isaiah 53? Read Acts 8:26-35 to see an example of the way Philip helped a man who could not understand this text.

4) Read once again the quote of Dr. Lloyd-Jones on page 36. Do you agree with what he says? How important is this for us?

6

Prayer for Spiritual Strengthening

Ephesians 3:14-21

In verse 14 Paul comes back to the point at which he digressed in verse 1. You will recall that the phrase, 'For this reason', is found in both these verses. It seems that his purpose at this point was the prayer that follows. This prayer closes the doctrinal section of the letter and introduces the wealth of practical application that is to follow in chapters 4 to 6.

'For this reason' refers to the great biblical doctrines taught in the first two chapters. Doctrine leads to prayer because doctrine opens up our understanding of God and that will inevitably lead to prayer. Don't let anyone tell you that doctrine is cold, academic stuff that dampens Christian enthusiasm. Doctrine is the truth about God and his gospel, and to contemplate such things as we have seen in the first two chapters must lead you to want to pray, to thank and praise God for such amazing love.

When Paul prayed to God the Father, he knelt (v. 14, and see also Acts 20:36). This revealed an attitude of reverence and wonder. There was no flippant familiarity with God but always the sense of the privilege of being allowed to come

39

before such a Being. The physical position of the body in prayer is not all that important, but the right attitude of reverence is. Most young people and new Christians find prayer rather difficult. Perhaps one of the reasons for this is a failure to appreciate the unspeakably great privilege it is to pray. In life we usually highly regard privileges and take every opportunity to benefit from them. We need to see prayer like that. Prayer is not simply talking with your eyes closed. It is speaking to your heavenly Father with your mind fully opened and aware of what great things he has done for you. It is a privilege purchased for you by Christ on the cross, so use it with reverence and joy.

THE CONTENT OF THIS PRAYER (3:16-19)

Bearing in mind that the prayer is in the light of the richness of the doctrine that has been taught, and in anticipation of the straight talking of application that is to follow, we can understand more fully the content of what Paul is praying for the Ephesians.

First, he prays that Christ may fill their hearts (vv. 16,17). On this point A.W. Pink says, 'The apostle prayed that the saints might have a spiritual sight of Christ, a spiritual knowledge of him, a spiritual enjoyment of him, so that he would be present and precious to the soul; and that can only be by an exercise of faith in him as he is revealed in the Scriptures. The apostle prayed for their hearts to be occupied with the excellency of his person, with his love and grace, with his blood and righteousness.'

The more clearly we see Christ, the more we will be willing to be instructed in the things God requires of us. The shallow Christian life is the product of a heart that has not properly understood the unsearchable riches of Christ. If you are not

40

living the Christian life as you should, it is always because you have forgotten the infinite price that was paid to make you a Christian. Young person, you have the grand privilege of demonstrating to a skeptical world the power of this gospel. There is no greater privilege in the universe.

Second, Paul prays that they may appreciate the love of God (vv. 17-19). If our lives are rooted in this love then they will produce the fruit of sanctified living that chapters 4-6 demand. Christ's love surpasses knowledge and yet we can know it, and must know it if we are to live lives worthy of our Savior. The dimensions of this love – its height, breadth, depth and length – are such that we can never exhaust it. There is always more to know and experience. Even in heaven we will go on learning more of this infinite love of Christ.

Living a Christian life is not simply a matter of self-discipline, though this comes into it; it is a life lived in response to God's love. It is as we know and appreciate this divine love that we will want to live to please him. Therefore, as A.W. Pink says, 'The chief spiritual employment of the Christian should be to live in consideration and admiration of the wonderful love of Christ, to dwell on it in his thoughts until his heart is warmed, until his soul overflows with praise, until his whole life is constrained or influenced. He should meditate daily on its characteristics; its freeness, its pureness, its unstintedness, its immutability'.

The great objective of this prayer is that the Ephesians, and we also, 'may be filled to the measure of the fullness of God'. This means that we may be saturated with God, and that our lives may more and more be emptied of self and filled to overflowing with the presence of God. It is to have as much of God as it is possible for a redeemed sinner to have. Our thinking, understanding and emotion are then captive to Jesus

Christ. It is so easy to be satisfied with little of Christ when we are offered such abundance in the gospel. Be ambitious in your expectations and look to know more and more of the love of God. It is an awesome adventure indeed.

The way to know more of God and his love is by knowing the spiritual strengthening that Paul speaks of in verse 16. To be spiritual men and women is totally alien to our fallen human nature, so we need the spiritual strength that only the Holy Spirit can give. He gives this strength not to our bodies but to our inner being. Dr. Lloyd-Jones says, 'The moment you begin to look into this inner man, and to analyse him, you see that he is very weak, very feeble, and needs to be strengthened. Were it not that we can offer for ourselves the prayer that Paul was offering for the Ephesians we should every one of us fail and falter. How often have we done so in mind or in heart or in will? If we were left to ourselves there would be no hope for us, and there would be no one to recommend the gospel. But thank God there is this way whereby we can be strengthened. The Apostle states it perfectly for us here. So that however weak you may feel yourself at this moment, however much you may have failed, this is the way. The Apostle's prayer is that "the Father of our Lord Jesus Christ, of whom the whole family in heaven and earth is named, would strengthen them in the inner man". May we not then say. All is well: I can be reinforced by God? I cannot make myself strong: I cannot put this iron into the walls of my soul; do what I will, I fail. But here is strength from God. He is all-sufficient!'

THE DOXOLOGY (3:20-21)

A doxology is a passionate expression of praise and confidence in God as the Christian realizes afresh the infinite love and power of the God he worships. Paul knows this. In his prayer he has been asking great things, and the question must be, is this prayer realistic? Is he asking too much? Has he let himself be carried away? His doxology answers these questions – *God is able!* It is this great truth that gives us confidence to pray. If God were only willing to help but unable to do so he would be just like us. But the Bible continually reminds us that God is able to do all things.

He is able to:

- Save   Hebrews 7:25
- Succor (help) Hebrews 2:18
- Subdue   Philippians 3:21
- Secure   2 Timothy 1:12
- Sanctify   Jude 24

Such ability, coupled with the love and grace of God we saw in the previous chapter, must give us great confidence and expectation to pray. We can never ask God too much. The words 'immeasurably more than we ask or imagine', are truly amazing. God is not only able to do what we ask, but even what we are afraid to ask. Blessings that for us only exist in our imagination are all within the power of God to provide. What a God!

The power of God is not something theoretical. Every Christian already knows something of it because it 'is at work within us'. We saw when we looked at Ephesians 1:19-20 that the New Testament yardstick by which power is measured is the resurrection of Christ. There is nothing greater than that. In the Old Testament the yardstick was the deliverance of Israel from Egypt – the Passover and particularly the crossing of the Red Sea. Time and time again the prophets in order to encourage people point them back to that event as a demonstration of divine power. But in the New Testament the empty tomb supersedes the Red Sea, and the same power that raised Christ from the dead has raised us from the grave of sin. This power is at work within us now. You couldn't be a Christian without the power of God. God's love and grace worked to save us but so too did his power.

In the light of all this, no wonder Paul concludes by offering praise to God: 'to him be glory in the church and in Christ Jesus throughout all generations, forever and ever! Amen.' The more you allow these truths to sink into your heart, the more you will be able to utter these words from the very depth of your heart.

QUESTIONS TO THINK ABOUT

1) What is your attitude to doctrine? Are you afraid of it? Do you think it is too hard to understand? Does it promote prayer in your life?

2) Why is prayer so difficult? What are the greatest obstacles to your prayer life? How are you seeking to overcome these?

3) Why are some professing Christians so shallow in their faith? How can this portion of Scripture address that problem?

4) Comparing the prayer of 3:14-19 with that of 1:17-19, how are they similar and how are they different? How does this prayer help you to pray for your fellow believers at home and church?

5) How does the doxology in 3:20,21 close the doctrinal section and prepare for the practical section of this letter? Do you act as if you really believe God is able to do all and more than you can ask or even imagine? If not, why?

7

Unity, Diversity and Effort

Ephesians 4:1-16

In the first three chapters Paul has been teaching us the doctrines of the Christian faith, but doctrine is not an end in itself. It is meant to be the basis and foundation of our new life in Christ. What we believe will govern what we do and Paul is saying that if we believe the doctrines already taught then we ought to be living the sort of life he sets before us in chapters 4-6. Doctrine and practice are inseparable in New Testament Christianity. Whenever there is a decline of interest in doctrine there will inevitably, sooner or later, be a decline in Christian behavior. The shallow evangelical life of today is the result of such a doctrinal decline. Some people think that you can have the Christian life without doctrine, but that is simply impossible. We cannot change the New Testament order of things without paying a deadly price.

If New Testament teaching is properly understood it will produce a life that honors and pleases God. By 'properly understood', I do not mean mere intellectual knowledge. It is possible to have all the right answers to theological questions but for those truths to leave the heart utterly unmoved. When that happens you are left with a cold, formal, loveless, proud orthodoxy that is as far removed from New Testament Christianity as liberal theology and humanism are. The right answers do not prove that doctrines are properly understood, but the right answers *plus* a right life do.

WALK WORTHY IN UNITY (4:1-6)

Doctrine is crucial and foundational but it is not enough, so Paul has to 'urge' (v. 1) and 'insist' (v. 17) that we put the doctrines into practice. As a young person do not be satisfied with knowing the truth. Your ambition ought to be to live the truth, and that is exactly what Paul is saying in verse 1. Once again he enforces his position by reminding his readers that he is 'a prisoner for the Lord'. He writes as one who has paid the price for his commitment to Christ.

In verse 2 Paul immediately tells us how we are to walk worthy of our calling. Humility, gentleness, patience and love are the main characteristics of a Christian life. These are all to do with our relationships with other people. If we are right with God then we ought to be right with each other. It is the absence of humility, gentleness, patience and love that cause tensions and quarrels, and inevitably will lead to a lack of unity in the church.

When we were saved God put us 'in Christ'. This is true of all believers, so there is a unity created by the Holy Spirit, that of being one in Christ. But if we do not live the life God expects from us we can and do break that unity. So Paul urges us to make every effort to keep it by being humble, gentle, patient and loving, which fosters a bond of peace. Work at this within your own age group in the church, but also with older folk whom you may consider to be living in the past. The tensions in churches between young and old believers can be quite devastating. Things like style of worship, type of hymns and songs, and versions of the Bible, can all shatter the unity of the Spirit if we fail to deal with them in humility, gentleness, patience and love.

When the New Testament talks of unity it does not mean uniformity. It is a unity based on the common belief in the doctrines of chapters 1-3, but there is more to it even than that. We are not told to be at unity only with those who believe exactly what we believe – that would be a very small church – but with those who are part of the 'one body' (v. 4). Stuart Olyott says, 'Do you sometimes look at other Christians and wonder how much you really have in common with them? We are such an assorted bunch! We come from different backgrounds and nations; we vary in intellect, achievement, social status and wealth; we represent a whole spectrum of characters, hang-ups and eccentricities, and express widely contrasting likes and dislikes! There are so many differences between us. What really do we have in common? All the distinctions we have mentioned are temporary. But there are seven eternal realities which we possess in common with all believers everywhere. What we share is immeasurably greater than what differentiates us. It is not logical that we should live in any form of disunity.'

These seven realities are spelt out for us in verses 4-6. All Christians have the same saving experience of the same Holy Spirit. One Lord has saved us and he has done so by giving us faith to believe in Christ. The phrase 'one baptism' causes some of us problems. Some of you will have been baptized by sprinkling of water when you were a child, others by immersion after you were saved; so there appear to be two baptisms. Because of this, baptism has become a great cause of disunity among Christians, but Paul is using it here as a reason for unity. This is because he is not talking about the mode of baptism but the fact that baptism always signifies identification with Christ. James M. Boice said, 'That is the unifying thing. Have you been baptized into Christ? I do not care how you were baptized. I do not care whether it was in a baptistry or a stream, whether it was with a little bit of water or in a lot of water. Have you been publicly identified with Jesus Christ? That is the issue. And if that is the issue, then before the world we are identified together with Jesus Christ and must stand together for him.' And finally, the seventh reality that binds us together with all the people of God everywhere in the world is that we all have 'one God and Father'. To focus upon these seven glorious realities will help us deal with the differences we have in every other area of life.

WALK WORTHY IN DIVERSITY (4:7-16)

All Christians do not have the same gifts and abilities (vv. 7 and 11). We are all different by God's design, yet the difference is not to affect our unity in Christ. Whatever gifts and abilities we have are given to us by the ascended Christ, and thus must never become a source of pride. They are given to us to work for the common aim 'that the body of Christ might be built up' (v. 12). He has called pastors and teachers, or pastor-teachers, to assist us in our growth. We must embrace them as gifts of the ascended Christ. It is a sad fact that many young people have little regard for the church and for its pastors. This is not how to grow to maturity. God wants mature Christians whose lives reflect the beauty of Christ (v. 13), and this will not happen if these gifted men are not respected and followed.

The opposite of spiritual maturity is infancy, and spiritual infancy is marked by instability and gullibility (v. 14). Of course, spiritual infancy is not necessarily true of only young believers. It has nothing to do with age, but with a doctrinal instability that leaves the believer open to all sorts of weird and dangerous viewpoints. Their beliefs are not dictated by the word of God but by any current opinion that is doing the rounds. Growth in the church is the product of spiritual growth in each individual Christian. We all have a part to play in the well-being of the church and we should be concerned that we promote growth and unity, not infancy and disunity. The young person in the church has as much a part to play in this as the older members. Do you promote unity in your church? After the service ends each week do you ever reach out to the older members and speak with them, or do you always stay in a huddle with those your own age? Are you seeking to be part of the solution, or are you content to remain part of the problem in the local church? May the Lord help you to see the vital place of unity in the body of Christ.

QUESTIONS TO THINK ABOUT

1) What is meant by the command 'to live a life worthy of the calling you have received'? How can this book of Scripture help you to fulfill this command?

2) What is the relationship between humility, gentleness, patience and love and the keeping of the unity of the Spirit?

3) How tolerant are you of those in the church who are different from you? How do you relate to those older than you, or those younger than you?

4) How do the unchangeable realities of verses 4-6 provide the foundation for true unity?

8

A Changed Life

Ephesians 4:17-32

By using the word 'insist' in verse 17 Paul is giving us no
option. There is no choice in this matter at hand. If we say we
are Christians then there must be evidence of this in how we
live. We are not to live as unbelievers do and as we once did
before we were saved by the powerful grace of God.

THE NEW MAN IN CHRIST (4:17-24)

One reason why Paul insists upon this is because of the nature
of salvation. He has already spelt out in chapter 2 what it
means to be a Christian. It is more than merely becoming
religious. It is the unique work of God in our hearts and souls.
We are new creatures in Christ; therefore we cannot live as we
once did. You cannot have Jesus as your Savior if he is not
also your Lord. Or to put it more theologically, it is the
relationship between justification and sanctification.

As you go on with Christ you will realize that the Lord has
done far more for you in salvation than you ever imagined or
hoped for. You came to Christ because of a conviction of sin
and a need for forgiveness. When you repented and received

Christ in faith as your Savior, you were forgiven and reconciled to the Lord. You were made acceptable to God in the Lord Jesus Christ. You were justified by faith and now have peace with God. This is glorious and thrilling, but there is more. Having justified us, God now begins in us the wondrous work of sanctification.

You may think that 'justification' and 'sanctification' are two rather heavy theological words that have very little to do with someone beginning the Christian life. If so, you could not be more wrong. You cannot be a Christian unless you have been justified, and the moment you have been justified the process of sanctification begins.

Justification is the sovereign work of God, whereby he declares the guilty sinner to be righteous and the rightful demands of the law satisfied so that all our sin has been dealt with in the way God's holy law had said it should be. The moment you are justified you are right with God. You could go to heaven there and then. You are accepted in Christ Jesus (Eph. 1:6, [NKJV]). But God does not stop there. He immediately begins in you the process of change, called sanctification, that will make you a different person. It will transform you more and more into the image of Jesus Christ. Justification frees you from the *guilt* of sin and its condemnation. It is a once-for-all declaration by God. Then, the moment you are justified, the process of sanctification begins which gradually frees us from the *power* of sin.

The difference between justification and sanctification can be summed up as follows:

1) Justification is all of God. Man plays no part. But whilst sanctification is also a work of God, it calls for the whole-hearted involvement of the one being sanctified. We

can only do this because God is working in us, but we must do it. We are not to be passive in this work, but fully active, as the entire teaching of the New Testament makes clear.

2) Justification is instantaneous; it is a once-for-all experience. You are as justified now as you will ever be, and you are as justified as any other Christian. Sanctification, however, is a process. It begins at salvation and goes on for the rest of our lives. The Christian can grow in sanctification, and he can also decline in it (what we call 'backsliding'). All Christians are at different stages of sanctification.

3) Justification makes us acceptable to God. Sanctification is to make us like Jesus. Union with Christ is the foundation of sanctification. It is because we are *in* Christ that we are called to be *like* Christ.

Salvation is like being pulled out of the raging sea when waves are about to engulf you and you have no hope. You have been saved and placed safely upon the rocks. The waves cannot harm you there. You are safe – safe on the Rock Christ Jesus. But salvation is more than a rescue operation. You must now go on to enjoy the life for which you were saved. You are on a rock, and in front of you is a seemingly unclimbable steep cliff. You realize you could no more climb that yourself than you could have got out of the water your own efforts. Again, I stress, you are safe on the rock, but you are called to go on and upward to a fuller life. The question is, how? Then you see a rope hanging down from the top of the cliff, and you hear a voice shouting instructions to you and saying, 'You climb and I will pull'. There may be many times when we feel that we can't hang on and our grip on the rope begins to loosen, but the Savior who rescued us will not allow that to happen. He has sent his Spirit to work within us what we cannot do alone.

That is sanctification. You are to climb over all the seemingly impossible obstacles that would try to keep you down, and at the same time God is drawing you upward and onward.

The second reason for Paul's insistence is because of who Jesus is. Jesus is the one who loved us when we were enemies. He died for us, and such a one deserves our obedience. He will only demand from us what is good for us, therefore the Lordship of Christ is most reasonable. It is demanding, but it is reasonable. We are not saved to do what we like, but to do what Jesus likes.

Paul works out his insistence in two ways: first in principle and then in practice. The principle is put before us in verses 22-24. We are called to put off our old self and put on the new self, or to lay aside the old ungodly habits and put on new godly habits. This again informs us that a conscious effort is needed if we are to change. It does not just happen; it has to be worked at. It is no good saying, 'I would like to be a better Christian – more spiritual and more prayerful'. You must do something about it. When you were saved that was all a work of grace. It had to be because you were spiritually dead. But that salvation involved a great change – you were born again. Now you are spiritually alive and therefore spiritual activity is possible. So there are things you must put off, but also ones you must put on.

Your old self is all that you were before you were saved. At that time self ruled, and your thoughts, ambitions and desires were all governed by this. But now you are a new man or woman in Christ, and he must reign. Righteousness and holiness are now to be the governing factors in your life. But you have got to work at it. Bad habits will not just go away – they have to be put to death and buried. Good habits will not just happen – they have to be cultivated. All this is not a matter of you by your own will-power turning over a new leaf; it is you by Spirit-power living the life that is possible in Christ and that pleases God. You must know that you still have a long way to go in the journey, but do not lose heart. The Lord is not only the Savior but the Keeper of his own.

THE DETAILS OF THIS NEW LIFE (4:25-32)

From verse 25 through the next chapter Paul works out in detail what he means. We will consider somewhat briefly here verses 25-32, and more fully 5:1-20 in the next chapter. You will notice that in these eight verses we are shown specific areas we are to put off the old ways and put on the new ways.

Verse 25. There must be no lying of any kind to any one, whether your parents, friends or anyone else. This is to be replaced with the truth for we are members of one another.
Verses 26,27. Anger is to be controlled at all times. There is a righteous anger, but we must beware of having this turn into unrighteous rage. The devil delights to see us go to bed with a grudge building in our hearts against someone. Don't do it!
Verse 28. There is to be no stealing of any kind from any one, whether from our parents, employers or the stores. Rather become a generous and diligent worker with your own hands. Laziness is to be replaced by diligence; dishonesty with honesty; and selfishness with generosity. This is the power of the gospel.
Verse 29. Be careful with your speech. Paul comes back to this again in Ephesians 5:4. John MacArthur says, 'Unwholesome language should be as repulsive to us as a rotten apple or spoiled piece of meat. Off colored jokes, profanity, dirty stories, vulgarity, double meanings, and every other form of corrupt talk should never cross our lips.' Instead we are to speak wholesome and life-giving words to build up those to whom we speak and to deepen the work of grace in their lives.

Verse 30. Behavior described in these verses grieves the Holy Sprit of God by whom we are sealed unto the day of redemption. It causes pain in the heart of God and it is inconceivable that any true believer should want to do that.
Verse 31. Notice that we are not to wait for things to happen. We are to take the initiative to rid ourselves of all bitterness, wrath, anger and all forms of malice.
Verse 32. This puts before us the opposite of the things listed in verse 31, and we are immediately back to what we were told in verse 2 with humility, gentleness, patience and love. If we simply apply this passage to all our relationships, especially in the home, we will see remarkable changes in us and those around us as well.

Some Christians think that it is legalism to insist on living like this. They could not be more wrong. Legalism is to be enslaved to man-made laws, but what we are dealing with here is the word of God. It is amazing how much sin is excused in Christians' lives by pleading legalism. Other Christians excuse themselves with pious-sounding words like, 'God has not convicted me of that'. But God does not need to convict us if he has clearly commanded us. Do not wait to be convicted about these things. This is the word of God, so do it!

QUESTIONS TO THINK ABOUT

1) Describe in your own words the difference between justification and sanctification.

2) What is the part you must play in your sanctification? How does Philippians 2:12,13 describe our duty and God's work?

3) How does Ephesians 4:25-32 help explain what it means to put off the old man and put on the new man?

4) How can we be guilty of grieving the Holy Spirit? What must we do to avoid this sad possibility?

9

Walk in Love, Light and Wisdom

Ephesians 5:1-20

All that Paul has been teaching in chapter 4 is summed up in the opening words of chapter 5: 'Be imitators of God.' This is an incredible command, but it is one that Jesus has already given in Matthew 5:48 and Luke 6:36. Clearly we cannot imitate God in power and might, and Paul is not asking us to.

WALK IN LOVE (5:1-7)

What Paul wants is that we walk in love, or 'live a life of love' (v. 2). We are to imitate Christ's love. This will be repeated in verse 25 with husbands particularly in mind, but in verse 2 Paul is addressing all believers with their sacred duty.

Love is to be at the heart of the Christian's life. It should characterize his thoughts, words and deeds. And it is such a love that gives value and purpose to everything he does. Christ's love was sacrificial (v. 2) and ours is to be like this, so immediately in verses 3-7 Paul deals with the opposite of such love which often masquerades as love in our world.

57

He minces no words as he deals with sexual immorality. The world has always mixed up love with lust. Lust is a totally sexual feeling whereas love controls all we are and do. The Ephesians' background was pagan religion in which sexual immorality was out in the open. We don't have that religious background but the culture of twenty-first-century Britain and America is exactly the same. In sexual terms anything goes. Young people have known nothing but this permissive philosophy so the warning is desperately needed. Today sex is big business – films, books, music and clothes all contribute to this. It is very difficult for a young Christian not to be tainted by it, but God's people are a holy people (v. 3) and among them there is not to be 'even a hint of sexual immorality.' Many young believers find sex a hard issue to deal with but this has always been the case. Nevertheless it must be dealt with and often the only remedy is to do what Joseph did when faced with his master's wife (read Gen. 39:6-12). He fled for his very life.

Some would argue that this is old-fashioned and there is no harm in free sex, especially today with all our pills and contraceptives. Paul's answer to this is, 'Let no one deceive you' (v. 6). Young Christians, you are to listen to God and not to an ungodly society. Take seriously the words of the Bible, not the empty words of vested interests and Christless hearts.

WALK IN LIGHT (5:8-15)

It is probably more difficult for youngsters to live a Christian life than it has been for many generations. This generation did not invent sex, but today it is so blatant in parading itself that its perversion is not even regarded as sin. Sex is a beautiful gift of God, but sin corrupts and disfigures it. Therefore it is crucial to know and apply verses 8-10. Christians are no longer in spiritual darkness. They are 'children of light', and therefore they are to walk in the light. We are told in verse 9 what this means. The characteristics of the Christian life are goodness, righteousness and truth.

Our business is to bring everything before the light of God's Word (vv. 13-14). It is God who decides what is right and wrong. There is no need for any believer to be confused on this matter – light always exposes darkness. John MacArthur says, 'Many commentators believe verse 14 is taken from an Easter hymn sung by the early church and used as an invitation to unbelievers who might have been in the congregation. The words are a capsule summary of the gospel. "Awake, sleeper" describes the sinner who is asleep in the darkness of sin and unaware of his lost condition and tragic destiny. Like a spiritual Rip Van Winkle, he will sleep through God's time of grace unless someone awakens him to his predicament and need. "Arise from the dead" is a summons to repentance, an appeal to turn away from the dead ways of sin. "Christ will shine on you" is the good news that God has provided a remedy for every sinful person who will come to him through his blessed Son, the Savior of mankind.'

WALK IN WISDOM (5:15-17)

This is the gospel by which we were saved and it is the pattern by which we are to live. There is only one way to live the Christian life, and that is *carefully* (v. 15). If you are careless or slack about your spiritual life you will get sucked into the world's way of thinking and acting. Being careful means being wise, and being wise means doing God's will (v. 17). Once again Dr. Lloyd-Jones helps us when he says, 'The Christian, because he is wise, is a man who has a correct view of life in this world and of the state of the world. He redeems the time because the days are evil. Nobody knows that but the Christian. To a non-Christian the days are wonderful; they have never been better... The days are not evil, there is plenty of work, plenty of money, plenty of everything. Ah, but the man who has wisdom is the man who says the days are evil. It is the wisdom of God alone that enables a man to say that'.

THE SPIRIT-FILLED LIFE (5:18-20)

The Christian life is more than just a matter of new behavior. It requires discipline and effort on our part, but these are useless without the enabling power of the Holy Spirit. Notice where Paul introduces the command to 'be filled with the Spirit.' It is not in the introduction to some great and difficult task only to be attempted by a few special Christians. It is in the middle of a list of everyday normal Christian behavior and relationships. In other words, the fullness of the Spirit is what every Christian needs in order to live an ordinary day-to-day Christian life. Without this fullness all other efforts we make will be doomed to failure.

It is true that sometimes the New Testament uses the phrase 'to be filled with the Spirit' to refer to what is needed in remarkable and special situations (Acts 2:4; 4:8,31). These verses refer to a filling for power. But in other verses, like Acts 6:3,5 it refers not to special actions but to a believer's normal condition. It is this use that Paul has in mind in Ephesians 5. The fullness of the Spirit is meant to be the every day experience of all believers if they are to be good husbands and wives, parents and children, masters and workmen.

It is interesting in verse 18 that before he tells us to be filled with the Spirit, Paul tells us not to be drunk on wine. There are some basic reasons why people get drunk. One is to escape from their problems. Pressures build up and they become depressed so their answer is to drown their sorrows. Secondly, they drink for pleasure, excitement and stimulation. A third reason is to conform to society, hence we get the term social drinking. Finally, people drink to give themselves courage to face a serious or frightening situation. It is in these ways that the man of the world deals with his problems.

The Christian has more than his fair share of problems, but he does not need to drink to cope with them. He has all the power of God working on his behalf. The more he knows of the fullness of the Holy Spirit, the more he will be able to face up to his difficulties and overcome them. Drunkenness leads to irresponsible action ('debauchery'), but being filled with the Spirit leads to praise, worship and gratitude. There could not be a greater contrast (vv. 19-20).

'Be filled with the Spirit' is not referring to a once-for-all experience but to a continual experience of being, as it were, topped up with the Spirit. The obvious question then is: *What must we do to get filled with the Spirit?* Stuart Olyott answers in this way: 'Verse 18 makes everything clear. How does a person get drunk with wine? He drinks and drinks and drinks again, until what he has drunk takes control. The same principle applies in the spiritual realm. We must drink spiritual things until we are under the Spirit's influence... Being constantly filled with the Spirit is a matter of constantly drinking. We are to go to Christ and drink of him. We do this in prayer, listening to biblical preaching, studying God's Word for ourselves, engaging in Christian fellowship, meeting around the Lord's Table, and in every form of spiritual and devotional exercise. As the Spirit does his work through these means, we become more spiritual people'.

We as Christians are called to live a life of love, as we walk in the light and avoid the deeds of darkness all around. We are to walk in wisdom, as we make the most of the time in the midst of an evil world, and we are to avoid being controlled by drink or drugs, but be filled continually with the Spirit of the living God. This is our challenge. Let us get on with it.

QUESTIONS TO THINK ABOUT

1) Paul opens chapter 5 with the command to imitate God. What are we to imitate, and how can this be done?

2) What is the difference between love and lust? In what ways does the world's view of love differ from the Bible's view?

3) What does Paul mean when he urges the Christian to walk in the light? How can the Christian expose the deeds of darkness as Paul admonishes in Ephesians 5:11?

4) What does it mean to walk in wisdom? How can we be sure we are making the most of every opportunity that God gives us?

5) How does a Christian obey the command to be filled with the Holy Spirit? Why does Paul contrast this to being drunk? Go back and read Stuart Olyott's words on page 61. Are you doing all you can do to see that you are filled with the Holy Spirit?

10

Spirit-Filled Relationships

Ephesians 5:21 - 6:9

Most of our Christian life is lived out in terms of relationships with other people and Paul lists three basic relationships that are to reflect the filling of the Holy Spirit: wives and husbands, children and parents, employees and employers. Every one of us has experienced at least one of these and most of us will be involved in all of them at some stage in our lives. Before actually going into the specific relationships the apostle seems to set forth a general principle in verse 21 that is to govern all our relationships: 'Submit to one another out of reverence for Christ.' He then applies this principle to the following areas:

WIVES AND HUSBANDS (5:22-33)

For some of my readers this relationship may still be a long way off. Nevertheless you cannot start too early in getting these biblical principles fixed in your mind. The breakdown of marriages today is frightening. It is an epidemic of tragic proportions. Christians as well as non-Christians get caught up in divorce, but this could largely be avoided if we knew and applied to ourselves the principles set before us here. We must take these things seriously. The tendency after reading a verse like this is for a lot of silly jokes to be made about the man being the boss and the little woman doing as she is told. The moment we do that, we denigrate the truth, don't take it seriously, the devil laughs, the Holy Spirit is grieved and we go off the rails.

There is a massive problem attached to marriage – both parties to it are always sinners. The potential for disaster that this can create is enormous, so how can any marriage work? The fact that many do should encourage us, and for the Christian we have the greatest possible encouragement in what Paul says here – but what a challenge it is! It is all put under the general instruction, as we have said, 'Submit to one another out of reverence for Christ' (v. 21).

This involves the husband loving his wife 'just as Christ loved the church', and the wife respecting her husband and submitting to him in everything. The love of the husband makes the submission of the wife possible. Her obedience and respect are a response to his love. Where one is lacking the other will find difficulty in surviving. So this is not all one-sided and basically involves both Christians in the marriage living a Christian life in the power of the Spirit.

A wife is not a servant but, as one for whom Christ has died, is equal with her husband before God. The husband's main function in the marriage is not to dominate and control the woman, but to love and care for her. And this love is to reflect Christ's love in that it is sacrificial, purifying and unbreakable. To this sort of love the wife should have no difficulty in submitting 'as to the Lord'.

If you are a young, unmarried person, now is the time for you to seek to become the person that God intends you to be for your future spouse. Are you even now praying for the right person to be led into your life, and are you seeking to become godly yourself?

CHILDREN AND PARENTS (6:1-4)

Do you have trouble with your parents and think that sometimes they have forgotten what it is to be young? Your children will probably be thinking the same thing about you in twenty years time! The generation gap never goes away and this makes it essential for the Christian to take these verses seriously. They transcend generations because they are God's will for his people in all ages. Because we hope this book finds it way into the hands of young people we will spend some time on these verses.

Youngsters today are being encouraged from many sources to rebel and do their own thing. But you as a Christian are told to *obey* your parents. You are not to argue, bicker or debate, but obey. The question is: why should you? Paul gives one simple answer: '... for this is right.'

It is right because common sense tells us so. Up to this point in your life no one has loved you as much as your parents. They have given you birth and ever since have loved you, prayed for you, worried about you and wept over you. The parent seeks only good for the child, whatever the child may think. For this reason alone obedience will nearly always work out for the good of the child.

The teenage years are often years of rebellion and youngsters greatly resent being told by their mother and father that they cannot do certain things or go to certain places or be with certain people. But they need to remember that the people who are telling them this are the ones who love them more than anyone else. Often this is a particular problem for children of Christian parents because you are not allowed to do what many of your friends do. Why is this? Is it because your parents are killjoys and don't like to see you enjoying yourselves? Is it because they are old fashioned and too strict? You know the answer to those questions. You have had too much fun with them to think they are killjoys, and had too many 'last chances' for you to think they are too strict.

Christian parents see their children as gifts from God, and they know they are responsible to God not only to care for the bodies and minds of their children, but also their souls. Some young people are allowed to swear, smoke, drink, stay out late and go anywhere, but not the children of Christians. This is because they are loved so much and valued so much.

Much more importantly, though, it is also right *because God commands it.* In verses 2-3 Paul quotes the fifth commandment and adds that it is 'the first commandment with a promise'. The promise is 'that it may go well with you and that you may enjoy long life on the earth'. Surely this should be enough for you if you are a Christian.

The obedience is to be 'in the Lord'. This does not mean if the parents are 'in the Lord'. It means that you, if you are a young believer, are to obey your parents as a service to the Lord. Colossians 3:20 says that such obedience 'pleases the Lord'. God is delighted to see it because it shows that young people are taking their Christian life seriously. Clearly God puts great value and importance upon your relationship with your parents.

Such obedience is not to be sullen, reluctant and forced. It is to be part of honoring your parents. To honor means to love and respect. God wants us not merely to do the right thing, but to do it with the right spirit. This may be very different from your friends' attitude to their parents, but that is the point. You are different. You are a Christian, so act like one in your relationship with both of your parents.

There are two problems that now need to be addressed. What are you to do if your parents are not Christians, and when, if ever, do you cease to be a child?

There is a tendency when faced with a clear and straight-forward command to look for reasons or excuses to make us exceptions. The command to obey your parents holds true even if your parents are not Christians. The only exception would be if they seek to make you do something that is contrary to God's Word. Obedience to God always supersedes everything else. But even then you must do so with great respect for your parents.

For many young Christians this can be difficult if they are converted in their teens and their parents are still unbelievers. The parents will be concerned at a change in their child that they do not understand. They may think that their son or daughter has gone too religious or has been brainwashed. How is the young Christian to behave in this situation? He must honor his parents as never before! He must not lash out at them or adopt a pious superiority over them. Their initial bewilderment is understandable and he must realize that. He must now, by his new life in Christ, show that he is a better child. He obeys and becomes more considerate and helpful around the home. In this way he is pleasing God and it is also a very effective method of evangelism. It shows that Christ really does make a difference to your life. And it is not unusual for unbelieving parents to be saved as they see the reality of Christ in their child's life.

What about 'adult children'? How long does this command to obey go on? What happens when the child gets married? Clearly the parents now do not have the same influence or control. In a sense honoring now lies more in care and concern and giving support when necessary.

There are some parents who are much easier to obey than others are. In this respect some young Christians have it much easier than others do, but the command still holds true. If you seek the help of the Lord and desire to obey you can do it.

So far we have been dealing with the child, but in verse 4 Paul addresses himself to fathers with the command that they are not to exasperate their children. In Colossians 3:21 he adds to this: 'Fathers, do not embitter your children, or they will become discouraged.' This exasperation can be caused in many ways, such as:

- Over-protecting children as much as neglecting them
- Inconsistency in the father's life, where he is one thing at church and another at home
- Failure to let children grow up, and, particularly in the teen years, to develop their own convictions
- Trying to relive his own childhood through his son

Fathers must be especially careful how they bring up their children, and children, as they see faults in how they were raised, must seek to avoid those same errors with their own children in the years to come.

EMPLOYEES AND EMPLOYERS (6:5-9)

Paul does not use the words 'employers' and 'employees' because obviously he is addressing the situation in his day, and 'masters' and 'slaves' are much more appropriate words. But for us today, we need to apply these verses to our situation and see them telling us how to behave at work, or for that matter, at school or college. Wherever we find ourselves, we are to behave as Christians. It is as simple as that – simple but not easy.

For a worker in an office or factory, it means you are not to be a clock-watcher, doing the minimum amount of work you can get away with. You are to work for your boss as you would work for Christ. For a student in school or college, it means you ought to be the best student in your class. You may not be the cleverest but you should be the hardest worker and the most attentive. In all this you are serving the Lord Christ, and from him you will receive the reward.

QUESTIONS TO THINK ABOUT

1) What is the massive problem in every marriage? What hope does Paul give in this section for the survival of marriage?

2) What is the relationship between the commands to husbands and wives and the filling of the Spirit in 5:18?

3) Why is it so difficult for children to obey their parents? What does Paul say that should motivate obedience to one's parents?

4) List several ways that parents can exasperate their children? What does Paul urge parents to do to counter this tendency?

5) Why should a Christian be the best student in class and the best worker on the job? What arguments does Paul use to help serve Christ in our employment?

11

The Armor of God

Ephesians 6:10-20

Several years ago I wrote a small book called *Stand Firm* that was a young Christian's guide to the armor of God. I would urge you to acquire and read that for a fuller explanation of these verses than I can give here.

THE ENEMY WE FACE (6:11,12,16)

Why is the Christian life such a battle? If God has done for us all that is described in the first three chapters of Ephesians, why do we struggle so much in the spiritual life, and why do we fail so often? The answer is given to us in Ephesians 6 verses 11,12 and 16. We have an enemy, one who is at work with all his energies to pull us down. That enemy is the devil.

The devil is no ordinary enemy. His power and influence are awesome; his armies span the whole world. Even Jesus calls him 'the prince of this world' (John 14:30). Many people today dismiss the whole idea of the devil as medieval nonsense, but Jesus spoke of him as a real person. If we take the Bible seriously, then we must take the reality of the devil seriously too. The Bible teaches that he is not merely an evil influence, but a real person. He is as real as God. Therefore to be able to deal with such an enemy we need all that God supplies for the battle.

THE ARMOR SUPPLIED FOR US (6:13-17)

The belt of truth. Paul is saying that truth is the first essential in fighting the devil. It is on this that the usefulness and the effectiveness of everything else depends. The belt signifies unqualified confidence in the truth of Scripture. This is the foundation of everything.

The breastplate of righteousness. What we need is a righteousness that is invulnerable, and this is exactly what God provides. When we are saved God imputes, or credits to us, his own perfect righteousness, and as we go on in the Christian life this righteousness is gradually being imparted to us by the inward work of the Holy Spirit. The difference between imputed and imparted righteousness is that imputed righteousness is all Christ's, and is perfect and absolute. It covers us and makes us acceptable to God forever. Imparted righteousness is the Holy Spirit making us more like Jesus. It is the continual work of God within us, and whilst in this life it will never make us perfect, it does make us more Christlike. It is this imparted righteousness that makes us hate all that the devil stands for. We are new creatures with a new Lord and Master, and we fight the evil we once embraced.

This, then, is the breastplate of righteousness that is going to protect our heart and all that flows from it, our feelings, our desires and our conscience.

The shoes of peace. The peace of God gives us stability and mobility in battle. We shall never know spiritual stability unless we learn to apply the truths and principles of Scripture to everyday living. If you are to live like a Christian, then you must learn to think like a Christian. And you will never think like a Christian unless you spend more time with Christ, who is our peace (Eph. 2:14). That means spending more time in prayer and Bible study.

If you have stability without mobility you will be like a lamp-post, stable, but cold; a lifeless pillar of concrete giving out light, but only in a very limited area. We need mobility so that the truth we know and love can move effectively against the enemy of our souls.

The shield of faith. How do we hold up the shield of faith? By quietly applying what we know and believe of the grace of God, so as to divert all the enemy's arrows. It is the application of the other pieces of the armor to the particular danger. Suddenly you are under attack. You must stand firm and respond quickly (the shoes) by applying the truth (the belt) and trusting solely upon the righteousness of Christ (the breastplate). Faith obviously includes what we believe, but it is more than that. Faith always acts, and its prime action is to point away from self to the love and grace of Almighty God.

The helmet of salvation. The purpose of the helmet is to protect the soldier's head. Thus Paul draws attention to the need in the spiritual battle for the protection of our brain, understanding and thinking. We discover the full meaning of the helmet of salvation in 1 Thessalonians 5:8: 'But since we belong to the day, let us be self-controlled, putting on faith and love as a breastplate, and the *hope of salvation* as a helmet.' In the New Testament the word 'hope' always points to the future, and it always means full and complete assurance. There is nothing uncertain about Christian hope. It is because we are saved now that we have the certain hope that not only shall we always be saved, but our salvation will be even more glorious when the Lord Jesus Christ comes again for his redeemed. Then our salvation will be final and complete; we shall be free not only from the guilt and consequences of sin, but also from its power and influence.

So when the devil comes to distort our understanding and depress us with thoughts of giving up the fight, we are to put on the helmet of the hope of salvation. We look past the present difficulties to the future glory.

The sword of the Spirit. The last piece of the armor is, strictly speaking, not part of the armor at all. Each of the other pieces is designed to protect a particular part of the body; they are all defensive. The sword, however, does not protect a particular part of the body, but the whole of the body; and it protects not by deadening a blow but by holding the enemy back. In addition, it is not merely defensive, but very much an offensive weapon; it can defeat and ultimately destroy the enemy. Paul calls it 'the sword of the Spirit', and then, to make absolutely sure that we know what he means, he adds, 'which is the word of God'. This sword, the only weapon of attack in our fight against Satan, is provided by the Holy Spirit, and it is the inspired, infallible, inerrant word of God. The Bible is crucial in the spiritual battle. We do not fight in our own strength; neither do we fight with our own weapons. Our own ideas and thoughts will be useless, but the Scriptures are part of the mighty power of God (v. 10). 'The weapons we fight with are not the weapons of the world. On the contrary, they have divine power to demolish strongholds' (2 Cor.10:4).

Our Lord modeled for us this use of the sword of the Spirit many times during his earthly ministry, but never more powerfully than during his temptation in the wilderness. He foiled the enemy by quoting the Scriptures (Matt. 4:1-11). Paul tells us in these verses that God supplies both the armor and the strength, and this he does for every Christian. Why then, if we all have the same resources, do some Christians fight the fight of faith and triumph, while others hardly fight at all and, when they do, melt like chocolate soldiers in the heat of battle? The answer is that, apart from anything else, the soldier must have two essential qualities to succeed: *discipline* and *endurance.*

DISCIPLINE AND ENDURANCE

The armor is available, but it has to be put on. It will not put itself on, and God will not put it on for us. Paul is very definite in Ephesians 6:11 and 13. The command is clear and crisp: 'Put on the full armor of God.' This is a matter of discipline and, of course, obedience.

When we have put on the whole armor of God we are able to stand firm and endure, and we will then be able to cope with all that the enemy throws at us. Paul encourages Timothy to 'Endure hardship with us like a good soldier of Christ Jesus' (2 Tim. 2:3). Endurance means staying power. Many Christians start off on their spiritual pilgrimage fizzing like a bottle of soda pop, but sadly all too soon they are flat like a bottle of water. Why was there no endurance, no standing firm? The probable answer is that they failed to put on the *whole* armor of God.

If you ever visit Windsor Castle in England, you will be able to see Henry VIII's armor. He was a big man, and he had a complete suit of armor specially made for him. The claim was, that, wearing this, he was invulnerable. Could you imagine Henry VIII charging into battle with his helmet on, and carrying his sword and shield, but still wearing his nightgown?

Of course not, that would be ridiculous! Yet many Christians do exactly that. You will not stand, I assure you, simply because you are saved. Neither will you stand merely by taking a great interest in the truth, or in faith, or in prayer. You need them ALL: not truth *or* faith *or* prayer, but truth *and* faith *and* prayer. There are Christians who are unshakeable on the truth of Scripture, but they are not much use as soldiers of the Lord because they do not know the true place and value of prayer. The opposite can also be true. It is possible to put a strong emphasis on prayer and give much time to it, and yet accomplish little or nothing in the battle. The reason is because such people neglect Scripture; thus they are easily deceived by the wiles of the devil. The only way to endure is with the whole armor on. Our strength comes from God, and we need the whole armor he provides for us.

THE VITAL PLACE OF PRAYER (6:18-20)

Paul's teaching on the armor of God does not finish with verse 17; he immediately goes on to show us how vital prayer is in the battle. Even though prayer is not part of the armor, it is indispensable to the success of the armor. This fact is captured well in the words of the familiar hymn by George Duffield, 'Stand up, Stand up for Jesus.' The second stanza reads as follows:

> Stand up, stand up for Jesus,
> Stand in His strength alone;
> The arm of flesh will fail you –
> Ye dare not trust your own.
> Put on the gospel armor,
> *Each piece put on with prayer;*
> Where duty calls, or danger,
> Be never wanting there.

Strength and power. What the armor represents – imputed righteousness, the hope of salvation, etc. – is great and glorious, but these things in and of themselves are not enough. We need strength and power to wear the armor, and that is only found in communion and fellowship with God, which, in turn, means prayer. You could saddle up a horse, strap a suit of armor to it and send it into battle. The armor is there in its completeness, but it will be useless. It is just an empty shell. We may as well not put on the armor at all if we think that God merely hands it out like some divine quartermaster in the sky. Our God is not like that. Neither is he like a car-hire firm merely providing a service. God does not hire his armor out, because without him it would be useless. In other words, Paul is telling us that we need the strength of God himself to fight this battle, not merely the armor he provides.

We must and ought to praise God for each piece of armor. They are all indispensable, but we need more than these. When Paul introduces the subject of prayer he is in effect only repeating what he has said in verse 10: 'Finally, be strong in the Lord and in his mighty power'. The word 'finally' tells us that everything that follows is only an elaboration of that. Putting on the full armor, together with prayer, is how we are able to 'be strong in the Lord and his mighty power'. We need to maintain personal, intimate fellowship with our heavenly Father and, for this, prayer is essential.

In the Christian life there is always a potential danger of becoming spiritually unbalanced. There are believers who really know the content of the Scriptures, but in the battle they are useless. They cannot apply the truth either in their own lives in sanctification or to unbelievers in evangelism. They know the truth, but there is no power, no life behind it. The reason invariably is a neglect of prayer. On the other hand, there are believers who spend hours in prayer, and they are useless in the battle, because of ignorance of God's revealed truth. Strength and power come from putting on the whole armor and infusing it with the life that comes only from prayer communion with Almighty God.

The battle is evidence of the power of sin, but the fact that we are still going on with the Lord is evidence of victory in many areas of our lives. We do not want to be complacent and indifferent to the many defeats we suffer, but neither do we want to minimize the work of grace that is going on within us. We must groan in repentance before God for the times when temptation overcomes us, but we must also learn to rejoice and praise the Lord when his power enables us to be victorious over temptation.

When we clothe ourselves with the armor of God, and are able to stand firm and triumph over the assaults of Satan, then victory has indeed a sweet taste. It is not the taste of pride, but of humility, for we are aware that in our own strength we are hopeless. Our victory is only because of our relationship to the Lord Jesus Christ. Nevertheless, God wants us to rejoice in it and daily offer our thanks and praise to him.

QUESTIONS TO THINK ABOUT

1) Why does Paul describe the Christian life as a battle? How are our enemies described in these verses?

2) Why is the belt of truth the first essential part of our armor?

3) What is the difference between imputed and imparted righteousness? How does this righteousness help us in the battle?

4) What is the remedy to prevent us from becoming spiritual lampposts? Why do you need all the armor to prevail?

5) What may we learn about the vital place of prayer in our spiritual battles? How do verses 19,20 help us understand how to pray for our spiritual leaders?

12

Ultimate Victory in Christ

Ephesians 6:21-24

Paul brings this glorious letter to a close in a customary manner that is found in most of his letters. He informs them of the faithful servant he has sent to tell them of his affairs and to comfort them concerning his well-being (vv. 21-22). He then closes with four key words that have been prominent throughout this letter: peace, love, faith and grace. He expresses his desire that the brethren, all the brethren, would enjoy the peace of God purchased at such a great price. He then desires that they would know both love and faith *from* 'God the Father and the Lord Jesus Christ'. He then places a final benediction of grace 'to all who love our Lord Jesus Christ with an undying love'. Such is the heart of this man who once believed with all his heart that he 'ought to do all that was possible to oppose the name of Jesus of Nazareth' (Acts 26:9).

THE ULTIMATE VICTORY

The great thing about the spiritual battle is that the victory is assured. The battle is ultimately between God and Satan. We are involved because we are Christians, but it is not *our* battle;

79

the battle is the Lord's. Satan is a mighty being, but God is almighty and invincible. This is why the victory is assured. In order to understand the nature of the victory, let us examine the nature of the battle. To do so we will draw an analogy between this battle and the battle for the Falklands in 1982.

On the Falkland Islands were living a community of men, women and children in peace. They were under the rule and protection of the British Crown, and they were happy to be so. But all that changed when an enemy invaded, imposing upon them a foreign rule and authority, and taking away their freedom. So far as the Falklanders were concerned, there was nothing they could do. They were too weak to resist, and their only hope was that Britain would value them enough to come to the rescue. This Britain did. Negotiations and talk proved hopeless, so a task force was sent; the enemy must be defeated and forced to withdraw. The cost of achieving this, in terms of lives and equipment, was enormous. Some argued that the price was too high and the Falklands were not worth it. But the price was paid. Lives were lost, victory was accomplished, and when freedom was restored to the islanders there was great rejoicing. The enemy, however, though defeated and humiliated, did not relinquish its claims to the Falklands, and so the threat still hangs over the victors. As well as that, the enemy left behind many minefields and booby traps, and these would be a potential source of danger for a long time to come. Of the victory there is no doubt, but the threat of danger is still there.

The world is God's creation, and he put man and woman in it to enjoy its beauty and to live for his glory. It was under God's authority and rule. Then Satan invaded with his great weapon of sin. Adam and Eve were soon defeated, and ever since the whole of mankind has been enslaved. Satan rules as the prince of this world. So far as man was concerned there was nothing that could be done; indeed, unlike those in the Falkland Islands, man became a willing captive. Our only hope was that the Lord would value us enough to come to the rescue. This God did. There were no negotiations. Satan, the enemy, must be defeated and man set free. But God sent no task force bristling with armaments. Instead, 'God sent his Son, born of a woman, born under the law, to redeem those under the law, that we might receive the full rights of sons' (Gal. 4:4). The cost to God was enormous; his Son must die to redeem guilty sinners. It could well be argued that the price was too high, and that sinners are not worth it. But still the Lord paid the price. Jesus died on Calvary and the victory was accomplished once for all time.

Salvation has been purchased for us by the precious blood of Jesus, and souls rejoice when they are saved. But Satan, though defeated, does not give up, and he continues to threaten the redeemed. As well as that, he still exerts an influence, because our old sinful nature is not dead and it acts like a spiritual minefield. Of victory there is no doubt, but the threat and danger are still there every moment of every day.

This is why we need the sort of truths we have seen in this wonderful book of Ephesians. When we can delight in these things then not only is victory assured, but even the battle becomes a daily opportunity to prove God and trust in him. Dear friend, I urge you to make this book of Ephesians your special companion, and you will find light to help you in the darkness of this world, and strength to enable you to make it through these most difficult years of your journey home.

QUESTIONS TO THINK ABOUT

1) How does Paul's heart for the Ephesian Christians manifest itself in the closing verses of this letter?

2) What special role did Paul entrust to Tychicus? Notice the similar language Paul uses in Colossians 4:7-9.

3) Compare the language of Ephesians 6:24 with that found in 1 Corinthians 16:22. Explain the vital place of love to Christ for the Christian. What can produce this 'undying love' within us?

Digging Deeper
into Ephesians

Digging Deeper into the Summary of Ephesians

For Personal Study

1. Go back and read the account in Acts 19:1 - 20:1 to see Paul's ministry in Ephesus. Becoming a Christian means a complete break with the old, sinful way of life led before conversion. How is this illustrated from this passage? (See especially vv. 18-20). Are there habits and practices in your life where similar drastic action is required?

2. Take time to read with great care Acts 20:17-38 where the Apostle Paul calls the elders of the church in Ephesus to come and see him one last time before he departs for Jerusalem. Describe Paul's ministry amongst them (vv. 17-27,31,34,35), and his challenge to them as the leaders of the church (vv. 28-31).

For Group Discussion

3. Read Revelation 2:1-7 and note the condition of this same church some years later after the martyrdom of Paul. What has happened to this church in the intervening years? How does such a thing happen to a church? Or to an individual? Ask the Lord to search your hearts as you are about to begin this study of the Epistle to the Ephesians. Consider how to be sure you do not leave your first love (1 Cor. 13; Jn. 14:15; 15:12; 1 Jn. 3:1-3).

For Prayerful Reflection

4. Read through the entire Epistle to the Ephesians at least once (preferably at one sitting) before beginning to read the various chapters of this book. There is no substitute for taking up the Bible for oneself and reading it with a humble and prayerful heart. Note the language of Isaiah 66:2: 'This is the one I esteem: he who is humble and contrite in spirit, and trembles at my word.' Pray that this will be your attitude as you begin this journey into God's holy word.

Digging Deeper into Ephesians 1:1-14

For Personal Study

1) Compare Paul's opening words to the Ephesians (1:1,2) with those in his other Epistles (Rom. 1:1-7; 1 Cor. 1:1-3; 2 Cor. 1:1,2; Gal. 1:1-4; Phil. 1:1,2). How are these similar? How different?

2) List at least seven times in verses 1-14 where 'in Christ' or 'in him' is used by Paul. Why is this phrase so important? Examine the following in this regard: Romans 8:1,39; 1 Corinthians 1:30; 2 Corinthians 5:17; Galatians 3:26-28; Colossians 1:27,28. How does this relate to Jesus' words in John 15:1-8?

For Group Discussion

3) Paul's burst of praise in 1:3-14 was originally one sentence in the Greek. Read this section aloud from as many translations as you have. Divide into three groups and have one consider the work of the Father, another the work of the Son and the third the work of the Holy Spirit in these verses. After you have had enough time, come together and discuss what you have found about the Trinitarian structure of this praise. How should this affect our worship and praise in church?

4) Election and predestination are clearly biblical doctrines, but many struggle accepting this. Why? How would you use Romans 9:6-24 to answer the objections that election is both unfair and removes human responsibility? How does Ephesians 1:3-6 help?

For Prayerful Reflection

5) From the MacArthur quote on the sealing of the Spirit, do you see these four primary qualities in your life? How can you go on strengthening these in your daily life? Spend time with the Lord in prayer, asking for help in seeing yourself clearly, and in determining to walk in obedience before him. If you are unclear about your standing before the Lord seek counsel from a pastor.

Digging Deeper into Ephesians 1:15-23

For Personal Study

1) Examine the prayers of Paul in some other letters(Rom. 1:8-10; 1 Cor. 1:4-9; Phil. 1:3-11; Col. 1:3-14; 1 Thess. 1:2,3) and compare them with his prayer in 1:16-19. How are they similar and how are they different? What do these prayers tell us about Paul as a pastor? Compare them with our Lord's prayer in John 17? Now compare these to your prayers. How can this help you pray?

2) Paul prays that the Ephesians would increase in their 'knowledge of [God].' Consider the following passages to see the vital place this knowledge has for us: Jeremiah 9:23-24; 31:31-34; Daniel 11:32; Hosea 4:1-6; 6:1-3; John 17:3; Romans 1:18-25; 2 Corinthians 4:6; Philippians 3:7-11; 1 John 2:4-6. List all you have learned about the knowledge of God from these passages.

For Group Discussion

3) Paul prays for three specific things in verses 18-19. Have one part of the group consider 'the hope...' (Rom. 8:18-25), another 'the inheritance...' (Gal. 3:26 - 4:7), and the third 'his incomparably great power...' (Eph. 3:20,21). Consider other portions of Scripture using a concordance to gain light on these verses, and then discuss your findings together.

4) As a group consider the central place of the resurrection of Christ in the New Testament. Have some consider its central place in the Gospels (Mark 8:31; 9:31; 10:33,34; 16:1-11), others in the book of Acts (1:3,21,22; 2:22-32; 4:8-12), and the rest in the Epistles (Rom. 1:1-4; 1 Cor. 15:1-22; 2 Cor. 4:11-15; Gal. 1:1) Discuss your findings together and consider how to use these truths in your evangelistic opportunities. Why does the book of Acts emphasize the resurrection of Christ even more than the crucifixion of Christ?

For Prayerful Reflection

5) Christ was raised from the dead, and seated in the heavenly places above every name that is named in all ages. All this was done that he might become head over the church, his body. Describe your attitude toward the church. Are you a member of a good church? Are you faithfully serving? Pray about your role in the church.

Digging Deeper into Ephesians 2:1-10

For Personal Study

1) Compare verses 1-3 with the description of fallen man found in the following passages: Genesis 6:5; 8:21; 1 Kings 8:46; Proverbs 20:9; Ecclesiastes 7:20,29; 9:3; Isaiah 64:6,7; Jeremiah 17:9,10; Matthew 15:17-20; John 8:42-44; Romans 1:18-32; 3:9-20. From these passages construct a defense of the doctrine of man's lost condition which you can use to witness to your friends .

2) In verse 3 Paul declares that we were once 'objects of [God's] wrath.' Study the doctrine of God's wrath from the following: Genesis 19:23-26; Exodus 12:29,30; Leviticus 10:1-7; Numbers 16:31-35; Deuteronomy 32:15-26; Luke 3:7-9; Romans 1:18; 2:5-9; 1 Thessalonians 1:10; 2 Thessalonians 1:6-10; Hebrews 12:29; Revelation 6:12-17; 20:11-15. Let us tremble before these words, and embrace Christ who alone delivers from the wrath to come.

For Group Discussion

3) Paul uses three great words in verses 4-9, 'mercy', 'love' and 'grace'. Divide into three groups assigning one word to each. You will have three passages supplied for each term; you search for more: *mercy* (Ex. 34:6,7; Ps. 89:1,2; Tit. 3:3-7), *love* (Isa. 43:1-7; Jer. 31:3; 1 Jn. 4:7-11), and *grace* (Acts 15:6-11; Rom. 5:19-21; 2 Cor. 8:9). Discuss together how these words should lead us to worship and serve God more faithfully.

4) As a group discuss the place of good works in the Christian life from verses 8-10. Examine Romans 4:1-8; 11:1-7; Galatians 3:1-11 and James 2:14-26. Relate James to Ephesians 2:8-10.

For Prayerful Reflection

5) Read back over these ten verses in private. Pause and ponder as you read verses 1-3, and ask yourself if this describes your *past* or your *present* condition. If they apply to your past, praise God right now. If this is still your present condition cry out for mercy in Christ.

Digging Deeper into Ephesians 2:11-22

For Personal Study

1) Consider carefully the five-fold predicament of the Gentiles described in verses 11-12. Take each term and trace other Scriptures that describe this dreadful condition. We will supply one for each, and you must search out the rest.
- 'separate from Christ' (2 Thess. 1:9)
- 'excluded from citizenship in Israel' (Matt. 10:5-7)
- 'foreigners to the covenants of the promise' (Deut. 7)
- 'without hope' (1 Thess. 4:13)
- 'without God in the world' (Acts 14:8-18)

2) Study carefully the central place of 'the blood of Christ' in Scripture. Examine Exodus 12:1-13; 29:9-21, Leviticus 17:11; Matthew 26:28; John 1:29; 6:53-56; Acts 20:28; Romans 3:25; 5:9; Hebrews 9:22; 10:19; 1 Peter 1:19; 1 John 1:7; Revelation 1:5; 5:9.

For Group Discussion

3) Discuss the meaning and significance of 'peace' as it is set forth in verses 14-18. Compare all the following passages in Paul's writings with these verses: Romans 1:7; 5:1; 8:6; 14:17,19; 16:20; 1 Corinthians 7:15; 14:33; 2 Corinthians 13:11; Galatians 5:22; 6:16; Ephesians 4:3; 6:15; Philippians 4:7,9; Colossians 1:20; 3:15; 1 Thessalonians 5:13,23; 2 Thessalonians 3:16. What is the role of Christ as 'Prince of Peace' in these passages?

4) Discuss the depth of the conflict between Jews and Gentiles at the time of Paul's writing. Numerous examples might be drawn from the Scriptures. How is this conflict still alive in the world today? What is the only hope for bringing true and lasting peace to these warring factions? Here are some examples, see if you can find some others:
Psalm 2:1-3; Luke 4:16-29; John 4:9; Acts 22:1-23

For Prayerful Reflection

5) Read again the last portion of our chapter under the heading 'Consequently.' Has the weight of this truth reached your heart? If so, take some time to reflect upon the pit from which you were dug, and offer heartfelt praise to the Lord. If not, then go back again and again until these truths melt your heart.

Digging Deeper into Ephesians 3:1-13

For Personal Study

1) In 3:1 the Apostle Paul refers to himself as 'the prisoner of Christ Jesus'. Search out the following verses to see how he spoke of his imprisonments, and how he responded to them: Acts 16:19-34; 20:22-24; 21:10-14; 24:24-27; 26:1-29; 28:30,31; 2 Corinthians 11:22-28; Ephesians 4:1; 6:19,20; Philippians 1:12-21. What enabled Paul to view his circumstances as he did? How might this help you as you face unwanted and disappointing circumstances in your life?

2) Paul uses the term 'mystery' three times in our section: verses 3,4,9, and three other times in Ephesians (1:9; 5:32; 6:19). Examine several other occurrences of this term in Paul's letters as you seek a fuller understanding of its meaning: Romans 11:25; 16:25; 1 Corinthians 13:2; 14:2; 15:51; Colossians 1:26,27; 2:2; 4:3; 2 Thessalonians 2:7; 1 Timothy 3:9,16. See also Matthew 13:11; Mark 4:11. A Bible Dictionary will be helpful here.

For Group Discussion

3) In verse 8 Paul refers to himself as 'less than the least of all God's people,' and the gospel as 'the unsearchable riches of Christ'. Divide into two groups and have one examine passages that describe Paul's view of himself, and the other his view of the gospel. After a sufficient time come back together and present your findings. Then discuss the intimate connection between his view of himself and of the gospel. How does this apply to us?
- Paul's view of himself (Rom. 7:14-24; 1 Cor. 3:5-9; 15:9,10; 1 Tim. 1:15)
- Paul's view of the gospel (Rom. 1:1-4,16,17; 1 Cor. 1:18-25; 2 Cor. 4:3-7; Gal. 1:6-10)

4) Discuss the vital place of the church in God's eternal plan. Begin with 3:10,11 and then consider 3:20,21; 4:15,16; 5:25-32; Colossians 1:18,24-29; Acts 20:28; 1 Timothy 3:14-16. How does the church display 'the manifold wisdom of God'? To whom? How does your local church display God's manifold wisdom?

For Prayerful Reflection

5) How precious is the privilege of prayer! Note the language used by Paul in verse 12: 'In him [Christ Jesus our Lord] and through faith in him we may approach God with freedom and confidence.' Compare this with 2:18: 'For through him [Christ] we both [Jew and Gentile] have access to the Father by one Spirit'. Take some time drinking in the thought that we have the opportunity and privilege of drawing near the Creator and Sustainer of the universe. Give thanks to God for this privilege, and thanks to Christ for making this possible.

Digging Deeper into Ephesians 3:14-21

For Personal Study

1) Paul says that he 'kneels before the Father' in verse 14. Does posture play any role in prayer? Consider the following verses as you think about this matter: Genesis 24:12-14; Exodus 34:8; Deuteronomy 9:25; Judges 20:26; 1 Kings 8:54; 1 Chronicles 29:20; Nehemiah 1:4; Psalm 63:4; Daniel 6:10; Matthew 26:39; Luke 18:13,14; John 17:1; Acts 20:36; 21:5. How do you pray?

2) Paul tells us he prays to 'the Father, from whom his whole family in heaven and earth derives its name'. How much do you make about having God as your Father? Examine the following to see what this means: Deuteronomy 32:3-6; Psalm 68:5; 89:26; 103:13; Proverbs 3:11,12; Isaiah 9:6; 63:16; 64:8; Malachi 1:6; 2:10; Matthew 5:16,45,48; 6:1,4,6,8,9,14,15,18,26,32; 7:11,21; Romans 8:15; 2 Corinthians 1:3; 6:18; Galatians 4:6; 1 John 3:1,2.

For Group Discussion

3) Paul's main burden for the Ephesians in 3:16-19 was for their spiritual strengthening. God is continually set forth as the source of strength for his people (Pss. 18:1,2,32; 46:1; 73:26;118:14), and at the same time the people of God are called to strengthen their brethren (Luke 22:32; Acts 15:32; Heb. 12:12). Divide into two groups and use a concordance to find at least 15 passages on each of these themes. How does our strengthening our brethren relate to God's strength? Close by looking back to Ephesians 1:19-21.

4) The reason Paul prays for their spiritual strengthening is that they 'may have power... to grasp how wide and long and high and deep is the love of Christ, and to know this love that surpasses knowledge.' Read aloud each of the following texts, and discuss together what it reveals of this infinite and unchangeable love of Christ: Matthew 26:36-46; Luke 23:39-43; John 13:1-17; Acts 7:54-60; 9:1-19; Romans 8:31-39; 2 Corinthians 5:14,15,21; 8:9; Ephesians 5:1,2; 1 Peter 2:21-25; 1 John 3:16; Revelation 1:4-7. Consider each passage separately and conclude with prayer.

For Prayerful Reflection

5) Paul concludes this chapter and this doctrinal portion of the letter with his most glorious doxology. Go back and read over prayerfully these words, and write them on the top of a blank piece of paper. Underneath these words write out the burdens you have pressing upon your heart at this time, whether they be for yourself or for others. List them one after another, and then look back at these words. Are they true? Do you believe that they are true? Take time now to cast each of these burdens into the strong arms of the Lord who 'cares for you' (1 Pet. 5:7).

Digging Deeper into Ephesians 4:1-16

For Personal Study

1) Read carefully the entire high priestly prayer of our Lord in John 17, and then come back and read Ephesians 4:1-6 in light of that prayer. Consider the place that unity and oneness are to have in the hearts and lives of God's people. Then pursue it!

2) 'Humility, gentleness, patience and love are the main characteristics of a Christian life.' If this statement is correct, then we must pursue these four virtues from the very start of our Christian life until the end. Study what the Bible says about these virtues, and start with the following:
- *Humility* (Ps. 25:9; Isa. 57:15; Mic. 6:8; Luke 18:14; 1 Pet. 5:5,6)
- *Gentleness* (Matt. 11:29; Gal. 5:23; Phil. 4:5; Jas. 3:17; 1 Pet. 3:4)
- *Patience* (Ps. 37:7; Eccles. 7:8,9; Heb. 6:12; Jas. 5:7-11; Rev. 1:9)
- *Love* (Matt. 5:43-48; John 13:34,35; Rom. 13:8-10; 1 Cor. 13)

For Group Discussion

3) Consider the 'seven realities' that are in verses 4-6: one body (1 Cor. 12); one Spirit (John 16:5-15); one hope (Heb. 6:13-20); one Lord (Rom. 14:5-13); one faith (Jude 3,4); one baptism (Rom. 6:1-10; 1 Cor. 12:13; Gal. 3:27); one God (1 Cor. 8:1-8). Discuss how these 'seven realities' can help us 'deal with the differences we have in every other area of life' in the church.

4) Apostles and prophets were given at the founding of the church, and evangelists and pastors and teachers for its growth through the ages. Read again verses 11-14 to see the role of the pastor and teacher in your life and that of the whole church. Study now 1 Timothy 3:1-16 and Acts 20:17-38 for more light on this role. Spend time praying for your pastors and teachers.

For Prayerful Reflection

5) Read verses 15-16 and focus on the words 'all... whole... every ... each.' Do you see yourself here? If you are a Christian you are there. Open your heart to the searchlight and seek the Lord for help to fill your unique place in the body. It's your duty!

Digging Deeper into Ephesians 4:17-32

For Personal Study

1) Paul 'insists' on a radical break from the former way of life that they followed in verses 17-19. When the deceitful mask is removed the ugliness of the world should repel us from following its ways. Examine the following and allow this picture to stir your soul: Proverbs 6:12-19; Matthew 15:10-20; John 8:42-47; Romans 1:18-32; 2 Corinthians 6:14-18; 2 Timothy 3:1-5.

2) Paul speaks passionately about the 'old self' and 'new self' in verses 20-24. Read that section once again and then turn to both Romans 6:1-14 and Colossians 3:1-11. Since these are the only three passages in the Bible that deal with these terms seek to grasp what is meant by them. Write your conclusions.

For Group Discussion

3) To distinguish between justification and sanctification is the first step towards becoming a sound theologian and Christian. Divide into two groups. Have one list all the ways that these great doctrines are similar and the other how they differ. Use the following passages to help: Romans 3:21-24,27-31; 4:1-8; 5:1-3; 6:11-14; 8:12-14,31-34; 12:1,2; Ephesians 2:8-10; Philippians 2:12,13; 1 Thessalonians 4:3-8; 5:23; Hebrews 12:14-16.

4) In verses 25-32 the apostle lists several virtues and vices that stand in opposition to one other. Divide into two groups, and have one group list the positive virtues that are to be pursued in seeking to 'put on the new self', and the other group those vices which are to be denied in seeking to 'put off the old self'.

For Prayerful Reflection

5) In verse 30 we are exhorted, 'Do not grieve the Holy Spirit of God.' Looking closely at the verses both before and after this command, ask yourself in what specific ways you have been guilty of grieving the Holy Spirit. Read Psalm 51:1-17 and seek to make it a prayer from your heart to the Lord.

Digging Deeper into Ephesians 5:21- 6:9

For Personal Study

1) The opening challenge of verse 1 is 'Be imitators of God.' Look back to 4:32 and forward to 5:1,2 to see what this means and how it is to be done. Note the wonderful phrase used to enforce this duty, 'as dearly loved children'. Look to the following passages to see how precious it is that such a phrase be used of sinners like us: Matthew 3:17; 17:5; Luke 20:13; Ephesians 1:6.

2) Verses 3-7 list several forbidden items for the Christian. These are hard words for young people today. Sex is big business and young people are bombarded daily on every hand. The media can dull the senses to the danger. Read again these verses and note the stern warning in verses 5,6. See Colossians 3:5-8.

For Group Discussion

3) Read once again verses 8-14, and note well the strong contrast between light and darkness. Compare the following passages to help clarify this imagery: Psalm 27:1; 36:9; 119:105; Matthew 5:14-16; Luke 11:33-36; John 3:19-21; 8:12; 9:1-5; 12:35-46; 2 Corinthians 4:4-6; 6:14; 1 Thessalonians 5:4-11; 1 John 1:5-7.

4) Walking in wisdom is the theme of verses 15-17. In order for young people to live wisely you must grow to 'understand what the will of the Lord is'. Study and discuss the following in this light: Psalm 40:8; 143:10; Matthew 6:10; 7:21-23; 12:46-50; John 7:17; 9:30-33; Acts 13:22; Ephesians 6:6; 1 Thessalonians 4:3-8; 5:18; Hebrews 13:20,21; 1 Peter 2:15; 4:1-3; 1 John 2:15-17. Discuss what you have learned about the 'will of God' from these passages. Learn it and do it!

For Prayerful Reflection

5) Read verses 18-20 and consider the importance of this call to be 'filled with the Holy Spirit' for your life. How does Paul's use of drunkenness relate to the control of the Spirit? Is your life marked by 'speaking... singing... [and] always giving thanks'? Be honest before the Lord and spend time in earnest prayer.

Digging Deeper into Ephesians 5:21 - 6:9

For Personal Study

1) Paul seems to prepare for this entire section on relationships by saying in verse 21, 'Submit to one another out of reverence for Christ.' How does this prepare for what follows? Examine each of the following places where the same Greek word translated 'submit' here is used: Romans 8:7,20; 13:1-5; 1 Corinthians 14:32-34; 15:27,28; 16:15,16; Ephesians 1:22; 5:22,24; Philippians 3:20,21; Colossians 3:18; Titus 2:3-5,9; 3:1; Hebrews 12:9; James 4:7; 1 Peter 2:13,18; 3:1,5,22; 5:5. How does the phrase 'out of reverence [or, fear] for Christ' both explain and enforce this command? Compare Psalm 103:11-14; Proverbs 1:7; 9:10; 2 Corinthians 7:1.

2) Study further the imagery of marriage and the relationship of Christ to his church from this passage. Make a list of the ways that Paul compares and contrasts these two relationships. How can this passage help young people approach marriage with the right attitude?

For Group Discussion

3) In 6:1-3 the children are directly addressed by the apostle. Notice that he does not speak *about* the children but *to* the children. He expected the children, whatever age, to be present in the assembly when the letter was read. As a young person how much have you made of these three verses directed to you? Read the following verses to enforce these words: Genesis 18:17-19; Exodus 20:12; Leviticus 19:;2,3; 20:7-9; Deuteronomy 5:16; Proverbs 1:8,9; 4:1-13.

4) In verses 5-9 the apostle gives very pointed instruction for all who are in a working environment. Look again at these words. Also read Colossians 3:22-25; 2 Thessalonians 3:6-15; 1 Peter 2:18-25. Divide into three groups and have each group examine carefully one of the above passages along with Ephesians 6:5-9. Make a list of principles that should be applied to your working relationship in the present and the future. How should a Christian worker differ from an unbeliever? Respond to the author's statement that as a Christian you are to be 'the best student in your class'? Do you agree? Explain your answer.

For Prayerful Reflection

5) As you consider your personal relationships in all the areas covered in these verses, how do you rate yourself at this time? How do you treat the opposite sex? If you are not married, are you developing the character qualities needed to fulfill God's Word? If you are married how often do you think about the way your marriage is a reflection of Christ and his church? Take time to pour your heart out to the Lord in this area.

Digging Deeper into Ephesians 6:10-20

For Personal Study

1) Read verses 10-13 once again and notice the number of commands that are pressed upon us: 'be strong', 'put on', 'take your stand', 'put on', 'stand'... Consider other places where this language is used and seek light to help understand our duty here: Deuteronomy 31:6,7,23; Joshua 1:6-9,18; 10:25; 2 Samuel 10:9-14; 1 Kings 2:1-4; 2 Chronicles 32:1-8; 2 Timothy 2:1.

2) Our adversary, the devil, stands opposed to us every day of our lives. In 2 Corinthians 2:11 the Apostle Paul states that 'we are not unaware of [Satan's] schemes.' Can you say the same thing? Are you alert to these wicked and deceitful schemes? Read and examine the following passages to see some of these schemes: Genesis 3:1-7; 1 Chronicles 21:1-8; Job 1:6 - 2:7; Zechariah 3:1,2; Matthew 4:1-11; 16:21-23; Mark 4:13-15; Luke 22:1-6,31,32; John 8:44; 13:2,27; Acts 5:1-5; 26:18; 1 Corinthians 5:5; 7:5; 2 Corinthians 11:14; 12:7; 1 Thessalonians 2:18; 1 Timothy 3:6,7; 5:15; 2 Timothy 2:26; Hebrews 2:14; James 4:7; 1 Peter 5:8; 1 John 3:8-10; Revelation 12:9; 20:2,10. One of the best ways to defeat an enemy is *to know the enemy*. Let us take this adversary seriously.

For Group Discussion

3) In verses 14-17 we are given all the specific instruments the Lord has provided for our spiritual warfare. Examine the following passages for more light on these verses: Isaiah 49:1,2; 59:15-20; Psalm 18:2,30,35; 28:7; 144:1,2; Proverbs 2:7,8; 30:5,6; Romans 13:11-14; 2 Corinthians 6:7; 10:3-5; 1 Thessalonians 5:8-11; Hebrews 4:12. Discuss together practical ways to encourage each other each day to be clothed with this full armor of God.

4) In verses 18-20 we are told of the vital place of prayer for our spiritual warfare. Divide into two groups and have one examine verse 18 and the other verses 19,20. Examine the following to help: Genesis 20:7,17,18; 32:22-30; Numbers 21:4-9; 1 Samuel 12:19-23; 2 Kings 6:8-18; 2 Chronicles 7:14; Job 42:10; Daniel 9:3-19; Mark 1:35; Luke 18:1-8; 1 Timothy 2:1-8.

For Prayerful Reflection

5) In the first three chapters the apostle tells us that we are 'seated' with Christ in the heavenly places. In chapters 4 and 5 he tells us that we are to 'walk' worthy of our calling by walking in love, light and wisdom. In this last section we are told to 'stand' against the wiles of the devil. Search your heart before the Lord, and honestly face yourself with the question: 'Am I walking in a way that pleases the Lord, and standing against the wiles of Satan?' Spend time in prayer about these vital issues.

Digging Deeper into Ephesians 6:21-24

For Personal Study

1) Compare the closing words here with those in several other epistles. How are they similar and how are they different? How do these closing words differ from the way you close your letters? What is especially striking about verses 21-24?

2) Paul was a man who placed a great deal of trust in his friends. In this letter he concludes by telling them that Tychicus was carrying the letter to inform them of Paul's condition. Write a brief biographical sheet on Tychicus from the following verses: Acts 20:1-6; Colossians 4:7-9; 2 Timothy 4:9-13; Titus 3:12-15.

For Group Discussion

3) Paul closes with four great words he desires for his brethren: *peace, love, faith* and *grace.* Divide into four groups and go back through the entire letter searching for all Paul said about each of these words. Take one word per group and then come together and discuss your findings. How are each one of these relevant for today's young person? How does the world define these terms? And where do they look for the fulfillment of each one?

4) Paul concludes with the words: 'Grace to all who love our Lord with an undying love'. The word translated 'undying' might also be translated 'in sincerity' or 'incorruptness.' Consider the other six occurrences of this word in the New Testament: Romans 2:7; 1 Corinthians 15:42,50,53,54; 2 Timothy 1:10. How does Paul's desire here relate to his closing words in 1 Corinthians 16:22? These two passages set forth the only two options for mankind. Close by reading Matthew 6:24.

For Prayerful Reflection

5) As you have now completed this study go back and look at the lessons the Lord has taught you throughout these weeks. What victories have you seen, and what set-backs have you had? Take time to give the Lord thanks for all you have learned, and close with a time of praise for having a Savior who answers every need you will ever have both here and into eternity! Hallelujah!

Selected Bibliography

Boice, James Montgomery. <u>Ephesians</u>, Baker Books

Jeffery, Peter. <u>Stand Firm</u>, Bryntirion Press (Wales)

Lloyd-Jones, Dr. Martyn. <u>Ephesians</u>, Banner of Truth Trust

MacArthur, John. <u>Ephesians</u>, Moody Press

Olyott, Stuart. <u>Alive in Christ</u>, Evangelical Press

Pink, A.W. <u>Gleanings from Paul</u>, Moody Press

Other Joint Publications from
Evangelical Press and Solid Ground Books

God's Outlaw: *The Story of William Tyndale and the English Bible* by Brian Edwards. A best-seller since first published in 1976, this book is now its 6th reprint. When Tyndale set out to provide the first printed New Testament in English he was forced to do so in defiance of the king, the pope and almost every person in authority. Compelled to flee from his homeland, he continued with his work of translating the Scriptures whilst slipping from city to city in Germany, Holland and Belgium in an attempt to avoid the agents who were sent from England to arrest him. His story is one of poverty, danger and ceaseless labor.

I Will Never be a Christian by Peter Jeffery. A powerful book to be given to the unconverted who have serious objections to the Christian faith. More than 12,000 copies have already been used set forth the case for Christianity to those outside the faith.

King of the Cannibals: *The Story of John G. Paton, Missionary to the New Hebrides* by Jim Cromarty. This is a wonderful book about a man of courage who trusted his God in spite of constant danger. Stuart Olyott says, 'No one can read this book and remain the same'. John MacArthur also says, 'Cromarty's lively writing style makes this a book that is hard to put down'. This is a great book to use in Family Worship.

Seeking God by Peter Jeffery. More than 50,000 copies of this powerful little book are now in print. This is a new reprint in an attractive booklet form that makes it inexpensive enough to buy quantities to give to the unconverted. Many people look back to the day they read this little book as the turning point in their lives. It contains the heart of the gospel in straightforward words.

Order on line from EP at sales@evangelicalpress.org
Order on line from SGB at solid-ground-books@juno.com
Order by phone from EP at 01325 380232
Order by phone from SGB at 205-443-0311